Revise for GCSE Geography AQA C

David Payne
Sue Jennings

Heinemann Educational Publishers
Halley Court, Jordan Hill, Oxford, OX2 8EJ
Part of Harcourt Education Ltd.

Heinemann is the registered trademark of Harcourt Education Ltd.

First published in 2003

07 06 05
10 9 8 7 6 5 4 3

British Library Cataloguing in Publication Data is available from the British Library on request.

ISBN 0435 09995 7

Edited by Catherine Matthews
Designed and typeset by AMR Ltd

Original illustrations © Harcourt Education Limited 2002

Illustrated by David Woodroffe

Cover photo: © Science Photolibrary/Bernard Edmaier

Printed and bound in the UK, by Bath Press

Picture research by Jane Hance

Acknowledgements
The publishers would like to thank the following for permission to reproduce copyright material:

Maps and extracts
pp. 9, 115 ©Crown copyright. Licence no. 100000230; **p.10** English Nature; **p. 17** ©*The Guardian* 11 September 1994 by Polly Ghazi, 20 November 1999 by Rory Carroll, 7 November 2000; **p. 35** Transport for London; **p. 53** US Agency for International Development; **p. 53** Christian Aid; **p. 61** Thames Barrier Visitor Centre; **p. 61** Extract from *Global Eye* No 8 published by Worldaware; **p. 67** *Understanding Global Issues* 7/92, European Schoolbooks Publishing Limited; **p. 69** Farm Africa,www.farmafrica.org.uk; **p. 71** Oxfam; **p. 76** © Bill Bryson. Extracted from *The Lost Continent* by Bill Bryson, published by Black Swan, a division of Transworld Publishers. All rights reserved; **p. 87** Extract from *World Poverty; Responding to Challenge* available from www.worldaware.org.uk/education/projects/wbg.html; **pp. 51, 87, 111** Extract from www.globaleye.org.uk, published by Worldaware; **p. 111** Rainforest Concern.

Photographs
p. 23 DJ Clark/ Panos, **p. 25** Crispin Hughes/ Panos, **p. 25** Maria Cuiza M Carvalho/ Panos, **p. 27** Jorgen Schytte/ Still Pics, **p. 35** Roger Scruton, **p. 66** Philip Maher/World Vision, **p. 70** Michael MacIntyre/ Hutchison, **p. 91** Michael Harvey/Panos, **p. 107** Author Photo, **p. 100** Science Photo Library/NASA.

Every effort has been made to contact copyright holders of material reproduced in this book. Any omissions will be rectified in subsequent printings if notice is given to the publishers.

Websites
On pages where you are directed to www.heinemann.co.uk/hotlinks for information, please insert the code 9957P at the website.

Contents

How to use this book

AQA Specification C

AQA Specification C is called an 'issues-based' specification because it looks at the way that issues affect people in different parts of the world.

The aim of the course is to:

- understand the background to a number of issues
- appreciate their impacts and consequences on people's lives
- consider the different ways that issues can be managed.

The specification is divided into three sections, each of which will be tested in the final examinations.

The three sections are:

- Managing change in the human environment
- Managing the physical environment
- Managing economic development.

These three sections are divided into four shorter units of study (chapters) as outlined below:

Managing change in the human environment	Managing the physical environment	Managing economic development
• Population change • Rural–urban migration in LEDCs • Changing city and town centres • Pressure at the rural–urban fringe	• Living with tectonic hazards • Weather hazards • Water and food supply • Pressures on the physical environment	• Contrasting levels of development • Resource depletion • Managing economic development • Tourism and the economy

Using this book effectively

This revision book has a number of features to help you prepare well for the final examinations:

- It is organized to reflect the examination specification, with three discrete sections, each containing four units of study (chapters) shown in the grid above.
- Each chapter has three double pages, which give background information and use case studies to develop human links to the particular issue
- At the beginning of each section there is a revision checklist made up of a series of key questions.
- At the end of each chapter there are helpful suggestions on how to improve your grade, **Making the grade**, and a number of practice examination questions (see the end of the book for a detailed mark scheme for each one).

Additional help

- **Key facts** and **Definition** boxes to help you identify the basic ideas and learn geographical terms.
- **Remember** boxes, to highlight important ideas or tips.

Remember

LEDC – Less Economically Developed Country
MEDC – More Economically Developed Country

Revision

- Know what is expected for each of the examination papers.
- Use the key questions on the revision checklists to organize your revision (pages 13, 47, 81).
- Make brief notes on each chapter to help you remember facts, and don't forget to **include examples** whenever you can.
- Use the practice examination questions and mark schemes to familiarize yourself with the style of questions, and understand how answers can be improved.
- Organize your revision into short units so that you can concentrate on small areas at a time.
- Try to find a quiet area to revise where you will not be disturbed.

The scheme of assessment

GCSE Geography (AQA C) consists of:

- **Coursework** – 25 per cent of total marks
- **Examination paper 1** – 25 per cent of total marks
- **Examination paper 2** – 50 per cent of total marks

Examination paper 1 (1½ hours long)

This paper is called a Decision Making Exercise (DME) and will be based on a topic which is published in advance.

The topic for 2003 will be: 'The reasons for change in the rural–urban fringe and the consequences of change for people, the environment and decision-makers. The paper will consider options about how one urban area might make use of its rural–urban fringe in the future.'

The topic for 2004 will be: 'An examination of the links between energy use and development and the potential impact of the use and development of energy resources. The paper will consider the finite nature of resources and the issues associated with the use of renewable sources of energy.'

See also the website for the AQA board on www.heinemann.co.uk/hotlinks.

Key points

1 For this paper you don't need to do a lot of revision, but you do need to do some preparation. The paper will test *skills*, *understanding* and *knowledge* of the topic area.

2 The paper will use a range of resources (this might include maps, diagrams, tables of figures, newspaper articles etc) to look at a particular topic.

3 The examination questions will be about:

a) using the information to show that you understand the topic

b) using the data and maps to test your mapping and graphing skills

c) using the data to test your interpretation skills

d) showing that you have knowledge of the chosen topic

e) making a decision and explaining carefully why you made it.

How to do well on this paper

1 Make sure you look at all of the information carefully. Make notes on the paper and underline/highlight parts if it helps you.

2 Be aware of what the questions are asking you and do what they ask.

In other words, if the question says 'Describe' – just describe or say what is in the information. If it says 'Explain' give some reasons.

For example, for a question about national parks: 'Suggest reasons for the increasing number of visitors to national parks'; your reply might be: *'More people have been visiting national parks because there has been an increase in car ownership and roads have improved, so access is better. Also, people have more holiday time today and many retired people would have the opportunity to visit areas like the Lake District.'*

There are three or four key points here and the answer shows a good level of understanding.

3 Read the questions carefully and write as much as you can. Use the mark allocation at the end of each question as a guide to how much you should write. One mark questions usually require a single point or sentence; four mark questions will require a number of points over a few lines. Never leave any questions blank. Even if you are not sure, always attempt an answer – you might score a few extra marks!

4 Show that you have studied the resources, perhaps by using appropriate quotes.

For example, suppose the question was:

'Describe how the number of people visiting the Lake District has changed.' (3 marks)

Resource:

Number of people visiting the Lake District			
1950	2 million	1980	8 million
1960	3 million	1990	9 million
1970	4 million	2000	10 million

A simple answer might be 'it went up'! While this is correct it would score only one mark. A better answer might be:
'From 1950 to 2000 the number of visitors went up from 2 million to 10 million, a rise of 8 million. It has increased every ten years, but the biggest increase was between 1970 and 1980 when it went up by 4 million.'

This answer makes several points and quotes/uses the information and would score all 3 marks.

5 Prepare by learning the skills required. This paper may include an Ordnance Survey map extract (1:50 000), so make sure that you revise your map-reading skills. These questions are often straightforward but answers **must** show a high level of accuracy.

Revise your map–reading skills on pages 114–115

Other skills that might be required:

- Describing and explaining information from photographs or newspaper articles
- Presenting information in a graphic form (line graph/ bar chart/ pie chart etc).

6 Finally, be prepared on the day of the examination. Come to the examination properly equipped with pens, pencils, rulers, rubber etc. Also, a few coloured pencils might be helpful.

Examination paper 2 (1¾ hours long)

Key points

1 This paper tests mainly knowledge and understanding of places and ideas, **so revision is vital**.

2 This paper tests the actual topics studied throughout the course which are as follows:

	Topic area	Revision checklist
A	Managing change in the human environment	Page 13
B	Managing the physical environment	Page 47
C	Managing economic development	Page 81

The paper will be organized into the three topics, with one question on each topic. Each question will be broken down into a number of parts, the marks for each part stated at the end of the question.

There is no question choice, so attempt every question. Even if you cannot think of an answer, have a guess – you have nothing to lose.

How to do well on this paper

1 You have 1¾ hours to do three questions, so you should spend about 35 minutes on each question.

2 Each question will have a number of parts – make sure you respond to the mark allocation, i.e. 1 mark = one sentence/point
6 marks = several sentences with examples.

3 Identify and respond to the command words. The most common command words are 'describe', 'explain', 'suggest reasons'.

4 Each question will have a number of resources with it. This might include maps, diagrams, figures, photographs, articles etc. (You may get an Ordnance Survey map extract at 1:50 000). You must use the resources to get as much information as possible – good use of the resources will get you many marks.

5 Each question will require an example, so detailed learning and case studies are important. An example of a question on this paper might be: 'In some places growing numbers of tourists put pressure on areas. Using examples you have studied explain how this might happen.' (6 marks)
A simple answer might be:

'When lots of people visit places on holiday they can cause problems with litter and it can make the place very overcrowded. Car parking is difficult and it takes a long time to get anywhere.'

This answer has two simple points but no examples and would therefore score about 2 marks.

A more developed answer might be:

'Thousands of people visit national parks or beach areas for holidays in the summer. Places like the Lake District National Park in NW England get real problems with traffic congestion and pollution. People leave rubbish about and footpaths are being eroded by all the walkers. In holiday places like the Isle of Wight (southern England) or the Mediterranean area many people visit in the summer and this puts pressure on water supplies and can create pollution in the sea because of the extra sewage. Also these places are getting really built up with lots of hotels which spoil the area.'

This answer has three named examples and a number of excellent points. It would therefore score 5–6 marks.

- It is best to use a small number of good examples rather than a lot of general points.
- When you use an example locate it well, i.e. a tourist area – The Lake District, North West England.
- You will always score marks for well-located examples.

6 Don't forget that you can use your local area, but if a local example is used it must be:

- well located
- appropriate to the question.

7 Answer every question – don't leave gaps, even if you are unsure. Always attempt an answer. You cannot lose marks for trying, and you will gain marks for anything that is correct.

Exam practice – Decision-making exercise

Paper 1

1 Study Figure 1.

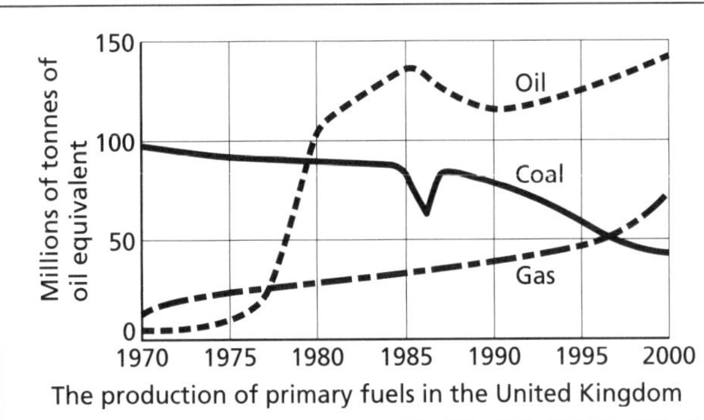

Electricity Demand (megawatts '000s)						
1970	1975	1980	1985	1990	1995	2000
36	40	43	45	46	47	50

◀ *Figure 1 The changing use of energy in the United Kingdom*

a) Describe the changes that have occurred in the use of oil, coal and gas. (3x2) (6 marks)

b) Construct a bar chart to show electricity demand from 1970–2000 . (4 marks)

c) Suggest reasons for the increase in the use of electricity between 1970–2000. (4 marks)

2 Study Figure 2.

SOLAR POWER
Solar power is expensive and not always useful in cloudy areas. The energy has to be stored, adding to the cost. It is clean and non-polluting.

MICRO-HYDRO
Small-scale systems are clean and non-polluting and electricity is cheap. However, they do require regular fast-flowing water and, if dams are required, the environment could be damaged.

WIND ENERGY
The United Kingdom has a lot of upland, windy areas suitable for wind energy. It is non-polluting but each turbine only produces a small amount of electricity, and they can be noisy and unattractive.

ENERGY FROM WASTE
Energy can be generated from household waste, although it is expensive and can cause pollution.

▲ *Figure 2 Alternative energy in the United Kingdom.*

a) Why are the types of energy shown in Figure 2 often referred to as 'renewable energy'? (2 marks)

b) Make a copy of the table below and complete it using Figure 2. (3x2) (6 marks)

	Advantages	Disadvantages
Solar Power		
Wind Energy		
Micro-hydro		

3 It has been suggested that a barrage could be built across the Severn Estuary between England and Wales to generate electricity. A part of this area is shown on Figure 3 (Ordnance Survey Extract).

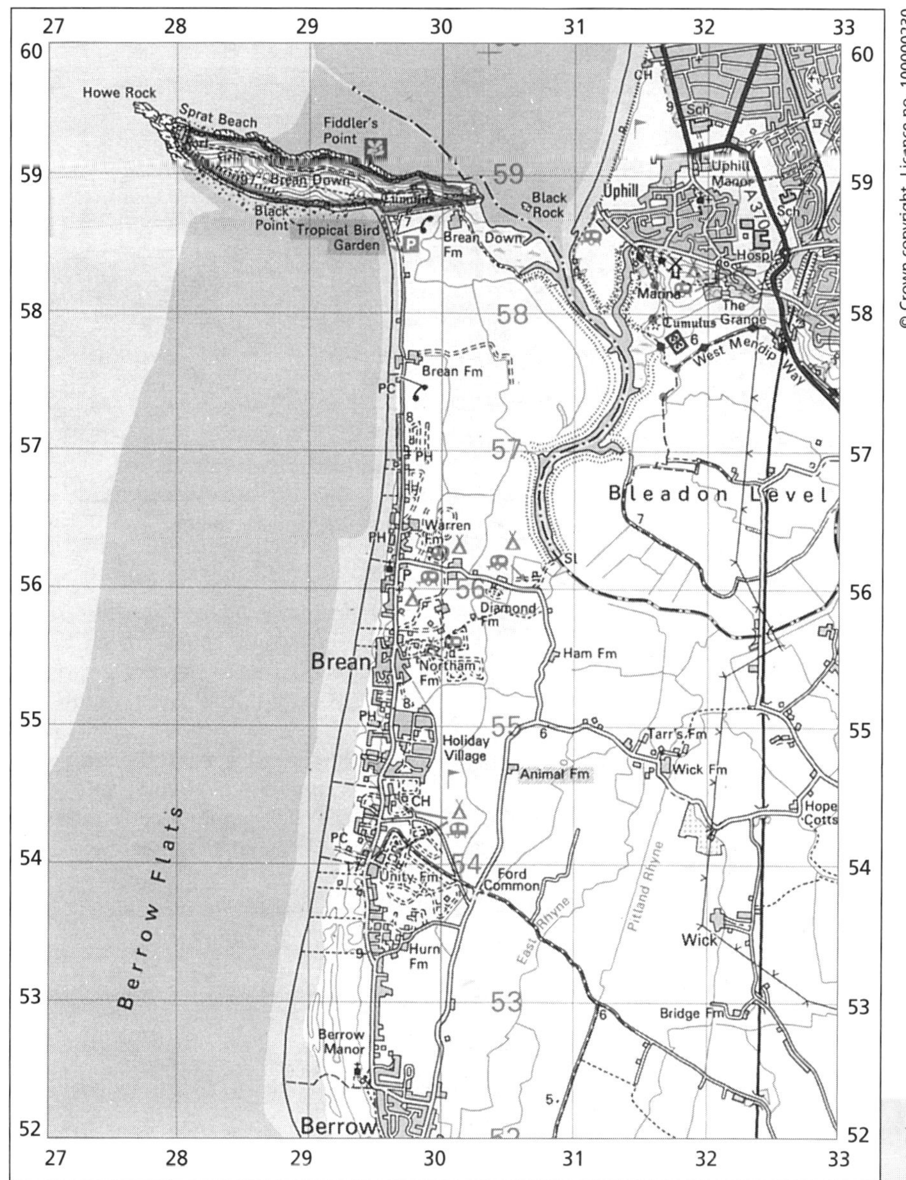

◀ *Figure 3 Extract from Ordnance Survey map*

a) **i)** Give the four figure reference for Wick Fm (farm) (1 mark)

ii) Give the six figure references for: Black Rock; Ham Fm (farm) (2 marks)

iii) What do the symbols represent at: 315594; 294525? (2 marks)

iv) Name two ways that height is shown on the map. (2 marks)

v) In which direction is Uphill Manor (3159) from Brean (2955)? (1 mark)

vi) Give the direct (straight line) distance from Black Rock to Ham Farm to the nearest km. (1 mark)

b) Use map evidence to suggest that this area is used by tourists. (4 marks)

c) Describe the physical geography in square 3157. (4 marks)

d) Why might the area on the map be environmentally sensitive? (4 marks)

Different views about the Severn Barrage

The Department of Energy

Electricity generation
Up to 7% of energy needs in the United Kingdom could be generated by the barrage.

Environmental effects
The development would affect sites designated for conservation reasons, but studies have shown that there are no environmental changes to these sites that could not be countered by various means, given that appropriate resources were made available.

Employment on barrage construction
Total employment would amount to some 200,000 man-years with a peak of about 35,000 jobs in the third year of construction. About half of these would relate to the local region. To this must be added the indirect employment generated by money passing into the economy from barrage-construction activities.

Employment as a consequence of the barrage
Following construction of the barrage it is estimated that there would be a build-up to an additional 10,000–40,000 permanent jobs in the region over the period 2001–2021, divided more or less equally between South Wales and the South West. These permanent jobs would comprise about 1,000 arising from the operation of the barrage and some 2,000 from increased tourism and the remainder from industrial, commercial and other activities.

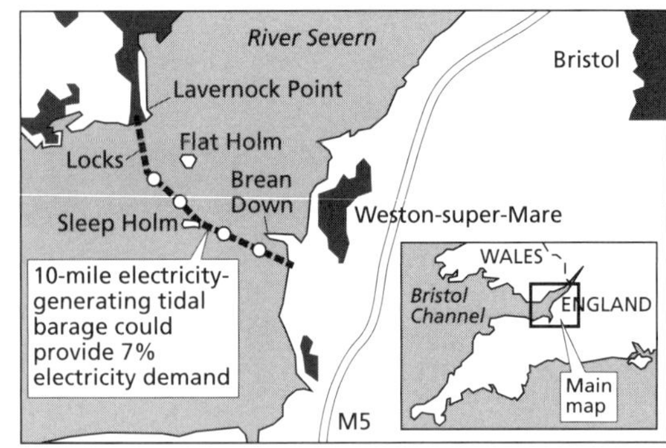

Increase in land and property values
Construction of the barrage would lead to an increase in land and property values.

Effects on ports
On the basis of present studies the effect of the barrage on local ports would appear to be broadly neutral but detailed modelling of shipping movements will be necessary to establish the true position.

Effects of the public road across the barrage
The economy of the South West, and more particularly of South Wales, would be assisted by the construction of a dual carriageway road across the estuary.

▲ *Figure 4(a) The Department of Energy's views*

The Nature Conservancy Council

1 Tidal power generating schemes have been, or are being, considered for many estuarine sites.

2 These sites support 63 per cent (750,000) of Britain's wintering wading birds. Other species use the estuaries during their long migrations to and from their wintering grounds as a safe place to moult and lose their feathers. Some, such as shelducks and redshanks, breed in important numbers on or near British estuaries.

3 The cost of constructing a tidal power barrage across the Severn Estuary, the most favourable site in the country, would be £5500 million. The 'useful' power output will be about 2 per cent of present demand because some of the power surges would come at times when little power is needed and cannot be stored.

4 The power would not be continuous, but would come in two pulses each day corresponding to a part of each tide period.

▲ *Figure 4(b) The Nature Conservancy Council's views*

Local views about the Severn Barrage

▲ *Figure 4(c) Local views*

4 Study the different views about the Severn Barrage, Figure 4(a–c).

a) Why might the barrage be a considerable economic boost to the area? (4 marks)

b) Explain why the development might create conflict in the area. (4 marks)

5 Do you think the Severn Barrage should be developed?

Explain the reasons for your decision, bearing in mind:

- The economic impacts
- The environmental impacts.

You may use any of the resources to help you. (9 marks)

Total (60 marks)

Section 1

Managing change in the human environment

Revision checklist

Use this page to check that you have covered everything you need to. If you can't answer any of the questions, go back to the relevant section.

1 Population change	• How do populations change in growth and age structures? • What are the physical and human factors that may cause these changes? • What are the effects of population change in LEDC and MEDC countries? • What are the impacts on people and resources of population change? • How can the causes and effects of population change be managed? • What are the likely effects of the methods of managing population change?
2 Rural–urban migration in LEDCs	• What is rural urban migration in an LEDC? • What are the push–pull factors that cause rural urban migration? • How does rural urban migration affect people's quality of life? • What are the problems that result from the growth of shantytowns? • How are urban housing and welfare improved in LEDC cities? • What are the advantages and disadvantages of improvement schemes?
3 Changing city and town centres	• How are town and city centres changing? • What are the causes of these changes? • What are the effects of changes for people, business and decision makers? • What are the environmental and economic effects? • What methods are used to manage change in MEDC cities? • What are the advantages and disadvantages of these methods?
4 Pressure at the rural–urban fringe	• How is the rural – urban fringe changing? • What are the causes of these changes? • What are the effects of the changes? • What is the involvement of government and pressure groups? • How are change and conflict in the rural–urban fringe managed? • What are the advantages and disadvantages of methods used to manage change?

1 Population change

How do populations change?

What has happened to the world population?

World population doubled between 1850 and 1950 and again between 1950 and 2000. In October 1999 world population reached 6 billion. In 2002 it was estimated that it had grown to 6.2 billion. It is predicted that this will rise to 10 billion by 2050. The annual world population growth rate or increase is 1.4 per cent.

The proportion of people in the world in LEDCs and MEDCs is changing so that a greater proportion of people are living in poorer, less developed countries and a smaller proportion of people are living in MEDCs.

The differences in population growth between MEDCs and LEDCs are shown in the table below:

World population	1950 2.5 billion	2000 6 billion	2050 possibly 9 billion
MEDC	0.8 billion 32%	1.3 billion 20%	Possibly 10%
LEDC	1.7 billion 68%	4.7 billion 80%	Possibly 90%

Definitions

Birth rate The number of births per 1000 people
Death rate The number of deaths per 1000 people
Fertility rate The number of births to women aged 15 to 45 (this gives a better picture of how many children are likely to be born in a country than the birth rate)
Infant mortality The number of children who die within the first year of life, per 1000
Life expectancy The average age a person can expect to live from birth
Rate of natural increase The difference between the birth rate and the death rate (more births than deaths will mean a population growth)
Migration The movement of people from one place to another
Population growth An increase in an area as a result of death rate, birth rate and life expectancy
Population change Change in a population measured in terms of birth rate, death rate and migration figures
Dependant population People who are too old or too young to look after themselves

Physical and human factors of population change

Physical factors:
- Natural disasters – floods (e.g. Bangladesh), earthquakes (e.g. Columbia), storms (e.g. Honduras)
- Disease – AIDS (e.g. South and East Africa).

Human factors:
- Healthcare
- Development
- Religion/culture (may encourage large or small families)
- Education
- Government (e.g. China)
- Conflict
- Migration (usually from LEDC to MEDC from poverty, persecution, disaster).

Remember

Physical and human factors can have different effects in LEDCs and MEDCs, for example good healthcare and high development levels in LEDCs will lead to a higher population growth rate in the short term as the death rate falls. In the long term populations will begin to reduce as birth rates also begin to fall, as is the case in MEDCs.

What is the pattern of population change over time?

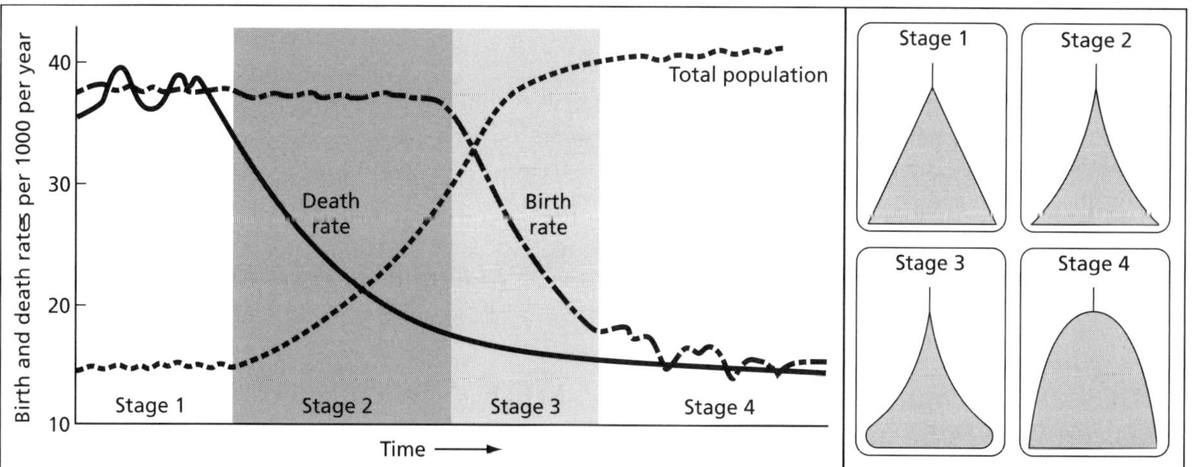

▲ *(a) The Demographic Transition Model and (b) population pyramids for the four stages* ▲

What are the causes of population changes?

The causes are physical or human or a mixture of both.

Stage 1 High birth rate, high death rate, low growth rate, stable population
Stage 2 High birth rate, death rate begins to fall, growth rate rises, population total rises
Stage 3 Death rate continues to fall, birth rate begins to fall, growth rate begins to slow down, total population rises
Stage 4 Death rate stays the same, birth rate falls, growth slows, total population may decline

The Demographic Transition Model (DTM) was devised to show how populations change as a country develops. The change may take 150 years (the UK) or 50 years (Japan). Countries are at different stages.

Remember

Populations change over time in structure, in distribution in the world and in density (how many people live in an area).

What is the population structure like in India now?

- The proportion of elderly people is small.
- There are an increasing number of middle-aged people.
- The proportion of young people under 15 is large.
- The total population will keep growing, typical of an LEDC.

What is the population structure like in the UK now?

- The proportion and number of older people is increasing.
- The number of young people under 15 is decreasing.
- The dependent population is increasing.
- The growth rate is static, typical of an MEDC.

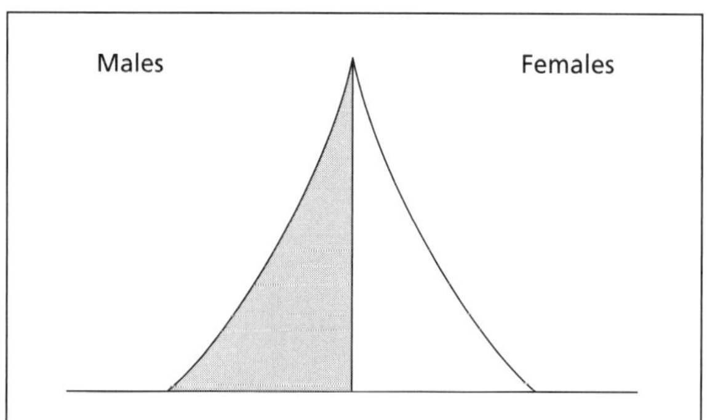

▲ *Population pyramid for India (LEDC)*

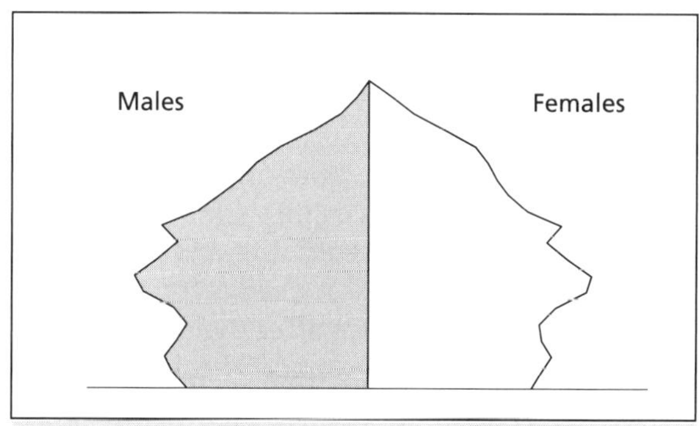

▲ *Population pyramid for the UK (MEDC)*

What are the effects of population change?

Population increase in MEDCs is very low but the population is aging with an increase in the proportion of older people and a smaller proportion of younger people. The rate of population increase is higher in LEDCs with a greater proportion of younger people and fewer elderly.

But patterns of population change have implications for resource use.

Key facts

- Changing age structures have impacts on people and resources in LEDCs and MEDCs.
- A high rate of growth (3–4 per cent) puts pressures on resources and the environment.
- Pressure on the land and rural resources will result in more rural–urban migration.

LEDCs – What could happen if growth rates continue to be high?

1 Basic necessities of life, such as food, water and fuel, will still be in short supply (as in Bangladesh today where the growth rate is declining).
2 By 2025, 2 out of every 3 people will have limited access to clean water.
3 More than 2 billion people will be hungry every day, with increasing levels of malnutrition, mostly in Africa and Asia.
4 Cities in LEDCs will continue to grow rapidly with high levels of pollution, disease and poor housing. Most mega-cities, such as Mumbai in India, are in LEDCs.
5 The quality of life may decrease with more dependent children and not enough work.
6 Adequate health care and education are difficult to provide for a rapidly growing population.

MEDCs – What could happen if growth rates continue to decline?

1 The proportion of dependent elderly people needing care will increase, as in the UK and Japan.
2 The number and proportion of young people will decrease, as in Italy.
3 The working population will be a smaller proportion of a country's population.
4 Services, such as healthcare and pensions, may be more difficult to provide for an increasingly elderly population.
5 Housing, education and other needs will change.
6 The quality of life for some may decrease, as in Russia.

Case study

Russia (MEDC)

Total population	145 million
Growth rate	–0.33%
Fertility rate	1.3 children/woman
Death rate	14 per 1000
Infant mortality	20 per 1000 births
Life expectancy	67 years

Few children are being born and there is a relatively high proportion of children dying within the first year of life. There is quite a high death rate and low life expectancy for an MEDC. The biggest need is for people to feel that they will be able to look after their children well and so have more children to support the ageing population.

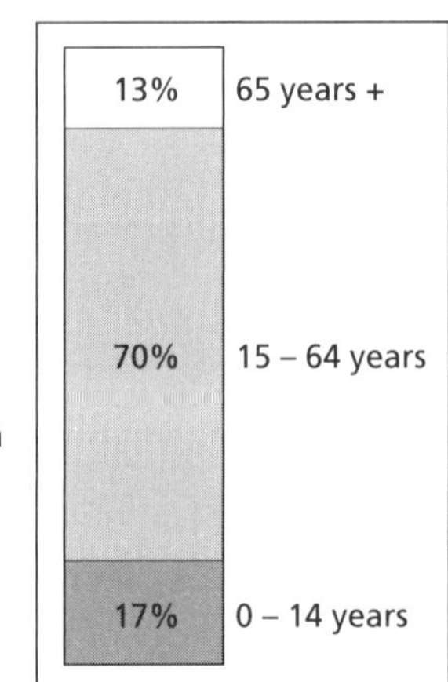

◀ *Population bar graph showing age groups for Russia*
Note: the age groups are the same for all four case studies (pages 16–17).

Case study

Bangladesh (LEDC)

Total population	133 million
Growth rate	1.6%
Fertility rate	2.72 per woman
Death rate	8.47 per 1000
Infant mortality rate	68 per 1000 births
Life expectancy	61 years

The birth rate is falling but the population will still increase as the 34 per cent under 14 grow up and have children. More resources, such as food, clean water, housing, healthcare, will be needed.

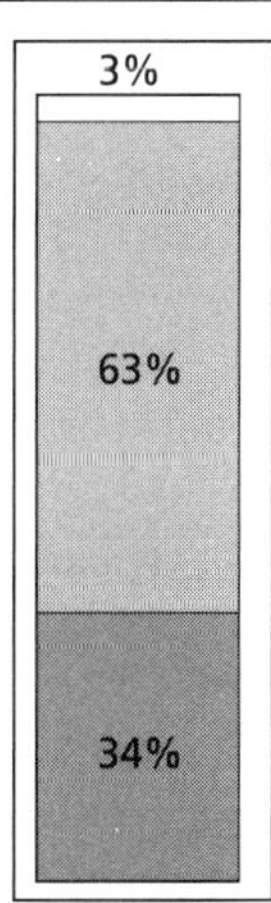

◀ *Population bar graph showing age groups for Bangladesh*

Fighting to hold back the flood

In Bangladesh, the world's most densely populated country, where 120 million people compete for space in an area the size of England and Wales, half of which is flooded most years, family planning has become an issue of national survival.

Almost half the country's married women use contraceptives and the move to smaller families is fostering a social revolution.

A generation ago few Bangladesh women worked. But a social revolution is following in the wake of family planning programmes, as tens of thousands of illiterate women receive rudimentary education which gives them a new-found status and power within the family.

Adapted from The Guardian, 11 September 1994

Case study

Italy (MEDC)

Total population	58 million
Growth rate	0.05%
Fertility rate	1.2 per woman
Death rate	10 per 1000
Infant mortality	6 per 1000 births
Life expectancy	80 years

The population is getting older and there are too few children being born to replace those dying or to be able to look after the old people in the future.

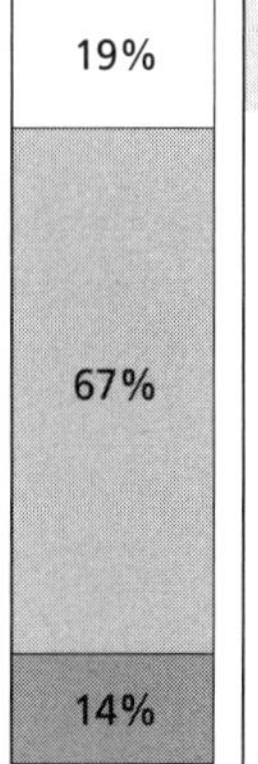

◀ *Population bar graph showing age groups for Italy*

Italy's baby crisis

Too busy hunting boar, making wine or playing football to settle down, the ageing bachelors of a dying Italian village have been catapulted into infamy by their mayor's ultimatum: marry or pay a singles' tax.

Vastogirardi, founded almost 2000 years ago on a mountain in southern Italy, will soon cease to exist unless its citizens start having children.

Mr Venditte, the mayor intends to levy a tax on the 50 men and 20 women who show no desire to marry or have children, despite prominently advertised government aid to families.

Many of the bachelors are part of Italy's army of so-called *mammoni*, grown-up sons who never leave their mothers and the comforts of home. Sociologists cannot agree on an explanation for the phenomenon, which carries no stigma in Italy.

Like their male counterparts, the village's new generation of educated, career-driven single women are in no rush to bag partners.

Adapted from The Guardian, 20 November 1999

Case study

Kenya (LEDC)

Total population	31 million
Growth rate	1%
Fertility rate	3.3 per woman
Death rate	15 per 1000
Infant mortality	62 per 1000 births
Life expectancy	47 years

Many of these figures are estimates because of the death rate from AIDS. AIDS can result in lower life expectancy, higher infant mortality and death rates, lower population and growth rates and changes in the population structure. The biggest need is for drugs and medical help to tackle the 2.2 million people living with AIDS. A birth control programme has been overtaken by the AIDS crisis. There are 220,000 refugees, most from Somalia and Sudan, in a country where food, clean water and shelter are in short supply.

3%
56%
41%

◀ *Population bar graph showing age groups for Kenya*

The effect of Aids in Kenya

Earlier this week the Kenyan Minister of State, Marsden Madoka, estimated that the AIDS pandemic was costing Kenya's barely solvent economy more than £1.8m a day in medical care, lost labour and funeral expenses. In less than five years the figure would be almost £17.5m a day, he said.

Government figures show that up to 25 per cent of Kenyans are HIV positive, but only 2 per cent can afford the recommended cocktail of anti-retroviral medicines. At about 432000 Kenyan shillings (£3800) for a year's course, the cost of treating all the infected Kenyans would exceed the national budget.

Adapted from The Guardian, 7 November 2000

Remember

Changes, such as, war, drought and famine, affect where and how people live.

How can population change be managed?

Both population growth and decline can be managed or controlled to a certain extent. Though population growth threatens LEDCs much more than population decline threatens MEDCs, they each bring their own problems. Without management it is difficult for MEDCs to maintain their quality of life and for LEDCs to improve their quality of life.

Why do we need to manage population change?

- Countries with too many people for their resources and a poor quality of life for their population may want to reduce the birth rate.
- Countries where only a few children are being born may have insufficient people in the future to look after the ageing population.
- Migration, because of war, natural hazards or for work, can affect population change. There are 13 million refugees and asylum seekers in the world today, 2 million in the EU.

What is the role of governments and NGOs?

Governments in LEDCs can influence family size by direct intervention (e.g. China), or by encouraging people to have fewer children (e.g. Bangladesh) or more children. NGOs, such as Population Concern and UNICEF, work to support people in improving the quality of their lives, for example they help with contraception for women in Bangladesh, and aid for subsistence farmers in Africa. This does have an effect on the number of children that are born.

Key facts

- Ways of managing population change may include birth control, provision of healthcare, education, agricultural reform and changes in employment.
- Governments and NGOs (non governmental organizations) have an effect on population change.

Case studies

The effect of government policies

LEDCs

China

The Chinese government decided in 1979 to enforce a one-child policy. Each family could have only one child because there would be famine and starvation if the population continued growing at the same rate. The policy was rigidly enforced and the population is, as predicted, now about 1300 million. The population will begin to fall around 2020. Most families want a male heir. Traditionally, a wife will stay with her husband and look after his parents. There are now many more men than women in China, 116 men to 100 females (2001 census). Some girl babies are abandoned and brought up in orphanages, but since 1999 families whose one child has grown up have been allowed to foster or adopt abandoned children.

India

With 1100 million people (2002) and 3.2 children per family, India may become the world's most populous country by 2020. The growth rate is slowing. The greatest fall in fertility is in the southern state of Kerala. Here women have always been valued and educated (85 per cent of women in Kerala are literate, 57 per cent in India as a whole), healthcare is good and infant mortality has dropped to 14 per 1000 (70 in India on average). Work is available and the social environment has changed. Families choose not to have many children, so the average is 1.8.

Aapted extract from The Guardian, mid-August 1994

How can some of the causes of population change be managed?

LEDCs

- **Birth control** Countries, such as Bangladesh, have actively encouraged people to have fewer children by providing information and contraception. China has enforced a one-child policy onto its population, but it may be possible to change the social environment, as in Kerala, India, which leads to parents wanting fewer children of their own accord.
- **Education** Educating women can contribute to a reduction in the birth rate (e.g. Kerala).
- **Agricultural reform** Changes in subsistence farming, such as the use of appropriate technology (e.g. Africa, Tools for Self Reliance), and agricultural reform (e.g Brazil) may improve yields and lessen stress on land and resources in rural areas.
- **Healthcare** Improved healthcare may help very poor people to see that they do not have to have six children to ensure that three will live long enough to help them in their work and look after them in their old age (e.g. Bangladesh).
- **Employment** Many people choose to have fewer children if they have work, money and their standard of living rises (e.g. Kerala, India).

	Kerala	India	UK
Life expectancy (women)	75	61	80
Infant mortality (per 1000)	14	70	6
Female literacy	85%	57%	99%
Average number of children per family	1.8	3.2	1.7

MEDCs

The main cause of population change in MEDCs is due to the fact that people are living longer and there is an ageing population, so it is largely this cause that has to be managed. Other causes of change are as follows:

- **Standard of living** If this falls in an MEDC and people become poorer, they may choose not to have children (e.g. Russia). If people think life will get better, they may have more children.
- **Choice** Some people just do not want children. The average family size is shrinking and in the UK is now 1.7 children per family, down from 2.4 in the mid 1990s. Governments may encourage their populations to have more children (e.g. in Italy).

How can some of the effects of population change be managed?

LEDCs

LEDCs have to plan for the provision of the basic necessities of life.

- **Food supplies, access to clean water, healthcare and education** can all be developed with the help of governments, NGOs (e.g. Save the Children, Oxfam) and foreign aid to improve the quality of life in rural areas and in squatter settlements in cities.

The way people live may change:

- **Migration** of workers to other countries (e.g. from the Philippines or Pakistan) means that money is sent back to the family left behind.
- **Agricultural change and reform** may enable people to feed large families (e.g. Kenya, India, Bangladesh)
- **The education of women** often leads to a smaller family size.

MEDCs

MEDCs have to plan for the provision of different services as a population ages (e.g. Italy, the UK, Japan).

- **Healthcare** is used more by older people than younger.
- **Housing** demands are changing, with a greater need for sheltered accommodation, retirement villages and more housing.
- **Employment** needs will change with the increase of the elderly, including their care.
- **Lifestyle changes** for older people may see a later retirement age, more leisure and travel.

Remember

LEDCs are greatly in debt to MEDCs, but poverty is the biggest influence on population change. Reduce poverty by taking away world debt and LEDCs will have more money to tackle healthcare, education and family planning.

Making the grade

Getting the most out of a graph

Your examination papers will include resources like graphs.

You may be asked to state or give information from the graph or to interpret trends or changes. You may be able to use information from a population graph in other questions referring to population change, ageing populations in MEDCs, changing inner cities or the rural–urban fringe.

Population pyramids

Population pyramids from contrasting regions in the UK 2001 census and the UK average.

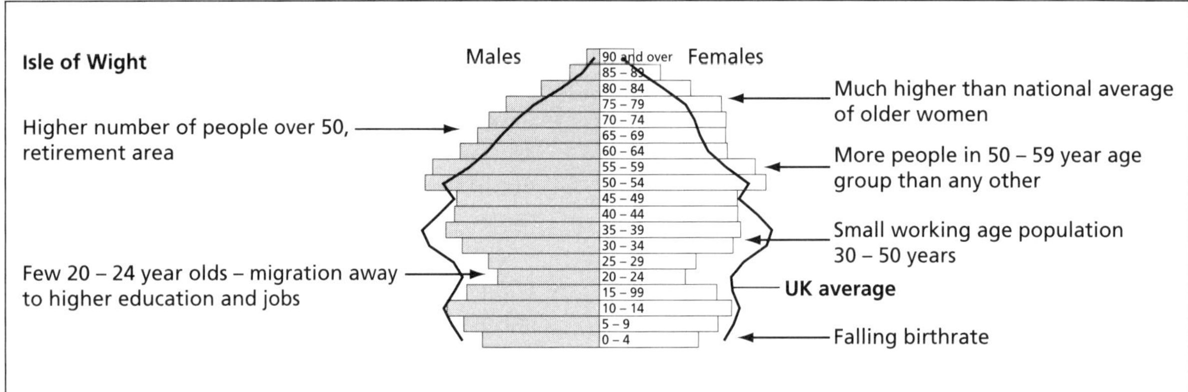

▲ *Figure 1 Population pyramid for the Isle of Wight, 2001 census*

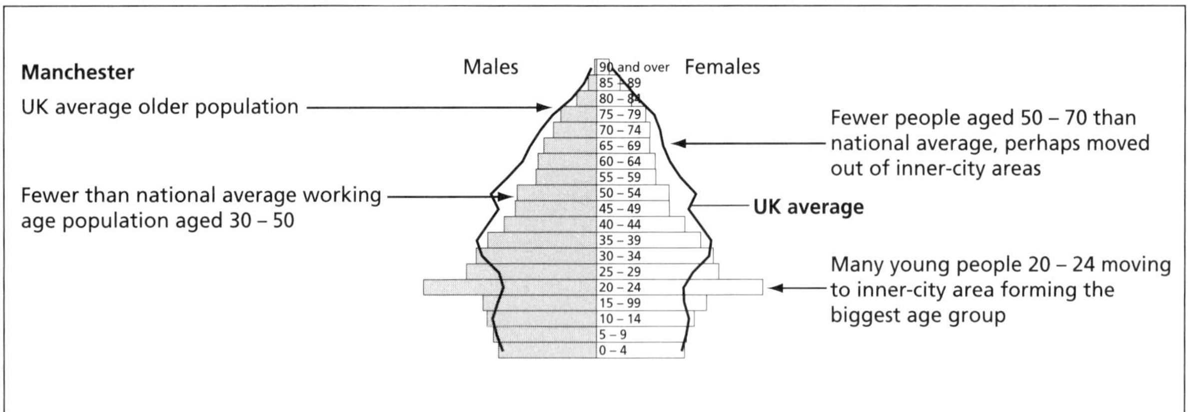

▲ *Figure 2 Population pyramid for Manchester, 2001 census*

Look at the differences between the population in the Isle of Wight and Manchester and the UK national average. Find the census details for your area and see if there are differences between the population in your area and the UK national average.

Exam practice questions

	Country	Birth rate (per 1000)	Death rate (per 1000)	Natural increase (Birth rate minus Death rate)
LEDCs	Bangladesh	35	12	23
	Brazil	25	/	18
	Egypt	29	8	
MEDCs	Japan	10	8	2
	United Kingdom	13	12	1
	France	13	10	

▲ *Figure 1*

1 Study Figure 1 which shows population information for some countries and complete 1(a) and (b).

a) Complete Figure 1 by filling in the natural increase for Egypt and France. (2 marks)

b) Use Figure 1 to select the right word in the following sentences.

A The natural increase in MEDCs is higher/lower then in LEDCs.

B Bangledesh/Brazil has the highest natural increase.

C The death rate is lowest in Egypt/Brazil. (3 marks)

2 a) What is migration? (1 mark)

b) Why are death rates low in MEDCs and some LEDCs? (4 marks)

c) Birth rates are higher in some countries than others. Using examples, suggest reasons why birth rates vary from country to country. (4 marks)

d) Migration may be caused by physical or human factors. Using examples, suggest reasons why people may migrate. (4 marks)

e) Describe the problems that may be caused by high levels of population growth in LEDCs. (6 marks)

f) Using examples, describe and explain how MEDCs are managing population change. (6 marks)

2 Rural–urban migration in LEDCs

Why do people move from rural to urban areas in LEDCs?

The world is becoming increasingly more urban with people moving to towns and cities every day. People who are attracted to cities are looking for new opportunities and a different and better life. The fastest growing cities are in LEDCs where most mega cities are found. By 2015 there will be 26 such cities in the world. About 2 billion people live in cities in Africa, Asia, the Middle East and Central and South America and the population is growing about 2.5 times as fast as rural populations.

▲ *The largest cities of the world*

Definitions

Push factors Things that encourage people to leave rural area
Pull factors Things that attract people to cities
Rural–urban migration The movement of people from rural areas to live in cities.
Urban growth The expansion of towns and cities.
Millionaire city A city with a million people
Mega city A city with over 10 million people

People who move from a rural area to a city are generally poor; they are pushed out by physical or human factors, and think life will be better in the city. Every year 5 per cent of the population of Bangladesh (5 million) think this and move to a city.

What is it about cities that people think will give them a better life?

Nearly 50 per cent of people in the world live in urban areas and this will grow to 75 per cent by 2025. The pull factors are what will draw them. Which order of importance would you put them in?

Pull factors
- **Work/employment/money** – may be easier to find in cities (e.g. São Paulo rather than in NE Brazil)
- **Healthcare/education** – though not great, are generally better in cities. The infant mortality rate tends to be lower and life expectancy longer
- **Food/water** – people think will be easier to find in cities
- **Protection** – seems better in cities away from conflict in the countryside
- **Quality of life** – is thought to be better in cities!

▶ *Pull factors to the city.*

What happens in rural areas to make people leave?

Push factors
- **Drought** – leaves subsistence farmers without food (e.g. East Africa)
- **Flooding** – wipes out homes and crops (e.g. Bangladesh)
- **Conflict** – may mean people leave the area suddenly (e.g. S Sudan).
- **Land degradation** – overgrazing and soil erosion reduce subsistence farming and contribute to famine (e.g. Kenya)
- **Population pressure** – one of the factors that encourage people to leave (e.g. Bangladesh averages 850 people per square kilometre)
- **Land ownership** – disputes and land division displace people
- **Mechanization of agriculture** – in sugar cane production has displaced thousands (e.g. SE Brazil)
- **Growth of commercial agriculture** – displaces subsistence farming (e.g. East Africa and SE Brazil)
- **Decline of traditional industries** – leaves people impoverished in many LEDCs

▲ *Push factors from the country*

Remember

Not all these factors apply to everybody. Combinations of events make people leave when they find the situation in the rural area so bad that the city has to be better.

Case study

Brazil: rural–urban migration

LEDC

Rural–urban migration to the cities on the coast has been important in the growth of Brazil. Many people in Rio de Janeiro or São Paulo, in the prosperous South East, have a high standard of living and life in a favela, an informal settlement where most people end up living, may seem more attractive than life in a destitute rural area. North East Brazil is the poorest region. There is little good land for small farmers and most farm labourers work in poor conditions, earning low wages on big estates growing sugar or cotton. The inland semi-desert (called Sertao) has frequent droughts and inadequate water supplies. There are few services and little employment. People frequently move to the cities on the coast in the South East.

▲ *Location map of Brazil*

▲ *The Sertao region*

What are the effects of rural–urban migration in LEDCs?

Cities grow because of migration, mostly rural to urban, and natural increase. The number of people who move to the city affects the whole city. People arriving from a rural area may first live on the edge of the city in a shelter made out of anything they can find, pallets, cardboard, mud, cloth. The roads into Mumbai, India are lined with temporary shelters and the pavement dwellers in Calcutta have been living in 'temporary' shelters for 20 years.

Shanty towns or informal settlements grow quickly on land not already used – on slopes where it is difficult to build (e.g. Rio de Janeiro), or on the most polluted, least desirable land (e.g. Nairobi). They may begin near the CBD, spread outwards over time as the city grows and become permanent suburbs (e.g. Rio de Janeiro) surrounded by a rapidly developing city. Many city problems are associated with informal settlements. The effects of rural–urban migration are not felt just in cities but also in the rural areas which change when people leave.

What are the problems in LEDC cities?

LEDC cities all suffer these problems, some worse than others.

Poverty – for most people in cities

Overcrowding – particularly bad in shanty towns with extended families living together

Clean water – scarce, often from a standpipe or bought at high cost

Sewage systems – inadequate or non-existent, tracks become open drains

Housing – made out of anything in shanty towns

Power supples – inadequate, often illegal

Pollution – of water, land and air is 'normal'

Traffic congestion – a problem for every LEDC city but shanty towns have especially poor road access

Rubbish – infrequently collected but may be recycled by local population

Violence and intimidation – common

Getting to work – difficult, expensive, and that is if work is available

Healthcare – scarce or expensive, disease spreads rapidly

Education – provision varies but shanty town children less well educated than other children.

LEDC city plans

The shape of most LEDC cities is irregular, with expensive housing near the CBD and the biggest area of land covered by shanty towns. Industry extends out along lines of communication, particularly roads, attracting more people. The pattern is different to MEDC cities.

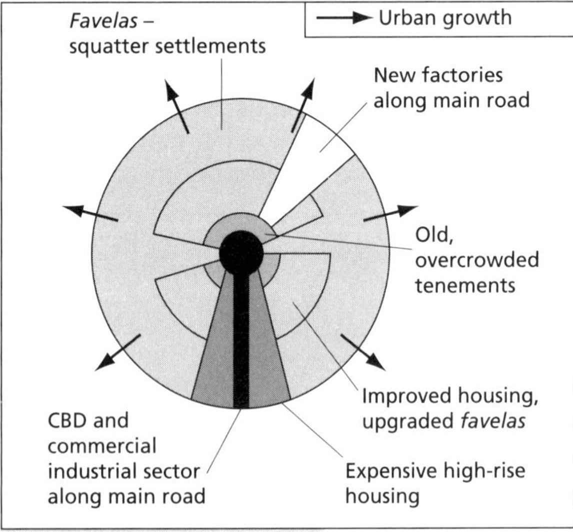

▲ *An LEDC city plan*

What happens to rural areas when people leave?

- Downward spiral of poverty for those left behind, particularly for the dependent old and young.
- Families may survive on money from workers who migrate to the cities.
- Commercial agriculture (e.g. in the sugar cane area of SE Brazil) can displace families and villages.

Case studies

Different types of shanty towns

▲ *A shanty town in Nairobi*

Nairobi, Kenya

Nairobi has a population of nearly 2 million people but the majority live in shanty towns around the CBD on land that floods easily. Rural urban migration in the 1900s and 1990s led to the growth of the city but the city is poor and work is scarce (50 per cent of the population of Kenya is unemployed). What are conditions like?

- Conditions are bad. Flimsy one-room homes are built from mud, boxes, polythene sheets and corrugated iron.
- Clean water is scarce, water shortages common.
- Crime and corruption are high.
- Open sewers run down the roads and overflow in the rainy season.
- Only 20 per cent of the rubbish in Nairobi is collected, though some people make a living by recycling it.
- Health care is poor, life expectancy is low and infant mortality rates high.

The government, NGOs and local people try to improve the quality of life but poverty is the biggest problem.

▲ *A shanty town in Rio de Janeiro*

Rio de Janeiro, Brazil

The population of Rio de Janeiro is 11 million, according to the 2000 estimate. Of that population 20 to 25 per cent live in favelas (shanty towns/informal settlements), a smaller proportion than in Nairobi.

Favelas grew most rapidly in the 1960s when they doubled in size and in the 1990s when there was a 60 per cent increase when many people left rural areas because of changes in the countryside. Early favelas were built on hillsides, but poor drainage, deforestation and erosion caused hillside collapse and every year people were killed.

What are favelas like? Homes in well-established favelas like Roçinha (100,000 people) are solidly built, but overcrowded and congested. There are some facilities – healthcare, shops and schools – but roads are narrow tracks and water and power supplies are scarce. Crime, air and water pollution are serious problems in Rio de Janeiro, but worse in the favelas.

Remember

Informal settlements vary from very squalid, frail constructions to almost permanent suburbs of cities.

How can living conditions be improved?

Conditions have been improved in some shanty towns, but it is extremely difficult to keep up with the enormous numbers of migrants from the rural areas. Changes in rural areas are necessary to reduce the flow of people to the cities.

Key facts

- Some shanty towns are old but have been improved (e.g. Rio de Janeiro, Brazil); some are newer and desperately need improvements (e.g. Nairobi, Kenya); some are large permanent slums where changes are difficult to make (e.g. Dharavi, Mumbai, India).
- People, individuals and groups try to improve living conditions.
- Authorities try to help with problems such as pollution, lack of water or sewage systems partly because of the impact on the rest of the city.
- Changes in rural areas could reduce the flow of people to the cities and so improve life for people in rural and urban areas.

Can people help themselves to a better life?

People can help themselves in small-scale ways by building homes or grouping together to run schools or clinics. They can borrow money to set up cooperative businesses and pressure the authorities to help.

How can authorities help people?

Authorities can:

- provide materials for people to build homes
- build low cost houses
- provide land for housing
- put in water supplies, toilet blocks and sewage systems
- deal with pollution.

What are the problems with government help?

There are, however, still many problems even if the government is willing to help:

- Only a few people may benefit from self build or low cost housing (e.g. Cingapora Project, São Paulo, Brazil).
- Few can afford the rent or mortgage and people are displaced to provide the land (e.g. São Paulo).
- Land provided by the authorities may be poor (e.g. along railway lines in Mumbai, India).
- Toilets, water pipes may generate health problems and corruption in water selling (e.g. Nairobi, Kenya).
- Sewage systems rarely keep up with urban growth (e.g. Cairo, Egypt).
- Crime and corruption put up costs everywhere.

Could changes be made in rural areas that would help cities?

The flow of people from rural areas could be reduced if life in the countryside improved with better healthcare, education, opportunities for employment, etc. The city might then seem less attractive.

The 'Green Revolution' was an attempt to increase food supplies in places such as India as improved strains of crops produced higher yields. Subsistence farmers need enough land and reliable water supplies. Some people suggest that land should be made available through land reform and commercial estates broken up. Probably 12 million people became landless in Brazil because of commercialization and mechanization of agriculture and most moved to the cities.

Case studies

LEDCs

Improving conditions in shanty towns in

Rio de Janeiro, Brazil

Rio is tackling big city problems, such as traffic congestion and air/water pollution as well as those in favelas (see map). Some favelas are 40 year-old successful communities of solidly built 3 or 4 storey houses with schools, shops and facilities, which are constantly upgraded by the residents. Many are on hillsides (which are unwanted for other development) with poor drainage. One problem is that deforestation and erosion cause the hillsides to collapse, killing people. Since 1980, favela residents and the authorities have run a reforestation, sewage, drainage and environmental education project together. Fruit trees and vegetables planted on the hillsides have prevented erosion, provided jobs, a better diet, stopped the hillside slipping and the harbour from filling with mud and reduced the costs of reinforcing work on the hillside. The authorities compensate the residents for the reforestation and work is managed in the community. All benefit.

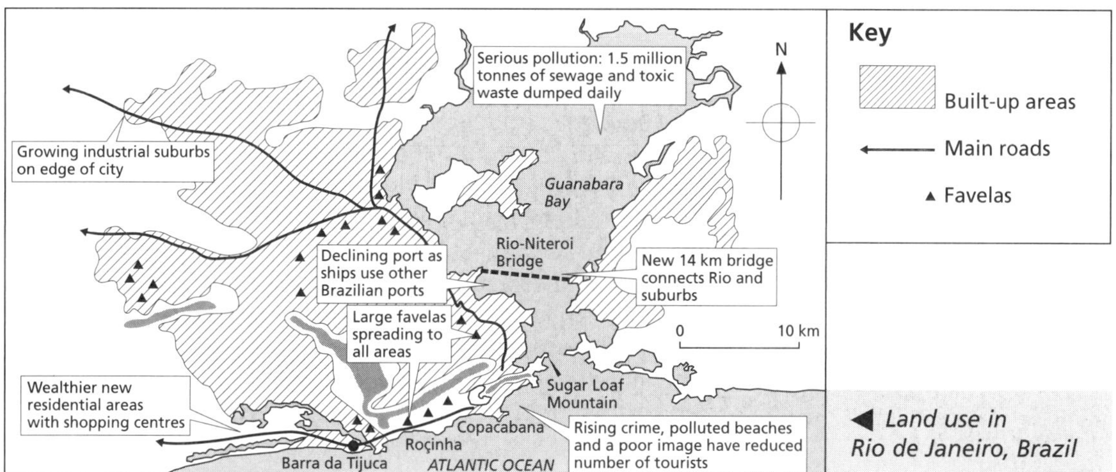

◀ *Land use in Rio de Janeiro, Brazil*

Nairobi, Kenya

Projects to provide basic amenities for five shanty town districts in Nairobi were supported by the World Bank in the 1980s. Water kiosks made water accessible and affordable to the poor but one kiosk may serve 50 families. Crime and corruption in water selling grew and water shortages are common. Toilet blocks were built but families had to share and health hazards increased. However, health has improved where sewers have been installed. Some low cost housing has been built but you need a job to pay the rent. Some informal work has been created. Urban services have improved but the city grows faster than the improvements as more people move from rural areas.

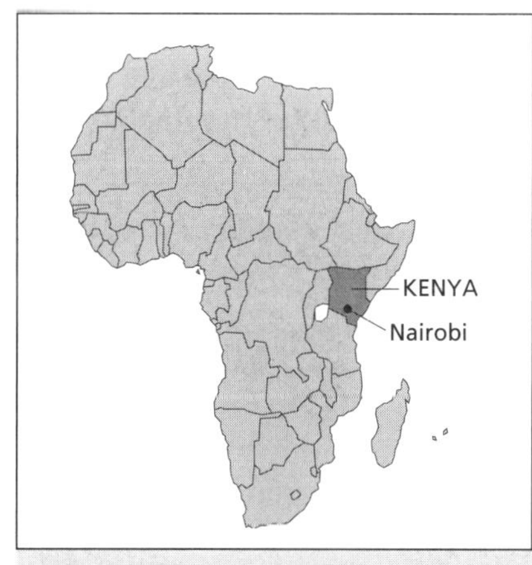

▲ *Location map of Nairobi*

▲ *A water kiosk in Nairobi*

Making the grade

Case studies

Case studies give you detailed information about particular events or places. You **must** use them when a question says 'use examples'. You can also use them in questions that ask you to describe, explain or suggest reasons for something.

How can you remember case studies?

	Revision example
1 What is the case study about?	Shanty towns (favelas) in South America
2 Where – location? **When – date/time?**	Hillside favela – Roçinha, Rio de Janeiro, South East Brazil, 1 km from sea What it is like now and how it has changed from its origins in 1960s/70s
3 What happened/causes? **Who is affected?** **How were things managed?**	Growth of favelas with rural–urban migration, e.g. Roçinha grew on hillside, unwanted land, surrounded by city growth Poor quality of life for 100 000 people. Problems include: • shortage of clean water • limited sewage system • brick and concrete housing but cramped and crowded houses piled on top of each other, widespread poverty • work mostly informal • limited services • restricted access to schools and healthcare • narrow tracks, limited vehicle access, goods carried by hand • corruption and crime. Problems managed by: • self-help schemes for house building • government help with low-cost housing, materials for self-build, some help with infrastructure, healthcare, schools • community help in hillside tree planting, typical of government, people and NGOs working together.
4 Which topics can I use this with?	You may be able to use case study data in different questions. Some of this case study could be used in a question on LEDC city problems and one on rural–urban migration or population change or levels of development.

Think locally

Try to make your own knowledge into a case study, perhaps using your local area. Ask yourself:

1 What is this case study about?
2 Where is it? What is the time span?
3 What has happened, who and what was affected and how were things managed?
4 Is this going to be useful for a question on several sections, e.g. the rural–urban fringe and population change, or changing city centres and recycling and resource use?

When you read an examination question, try to jot down rough brief notes about a case study that you can use, **selecting only the data relevant to the question**. Do not write down all you know without relating the information to the question.

Exam practice questions

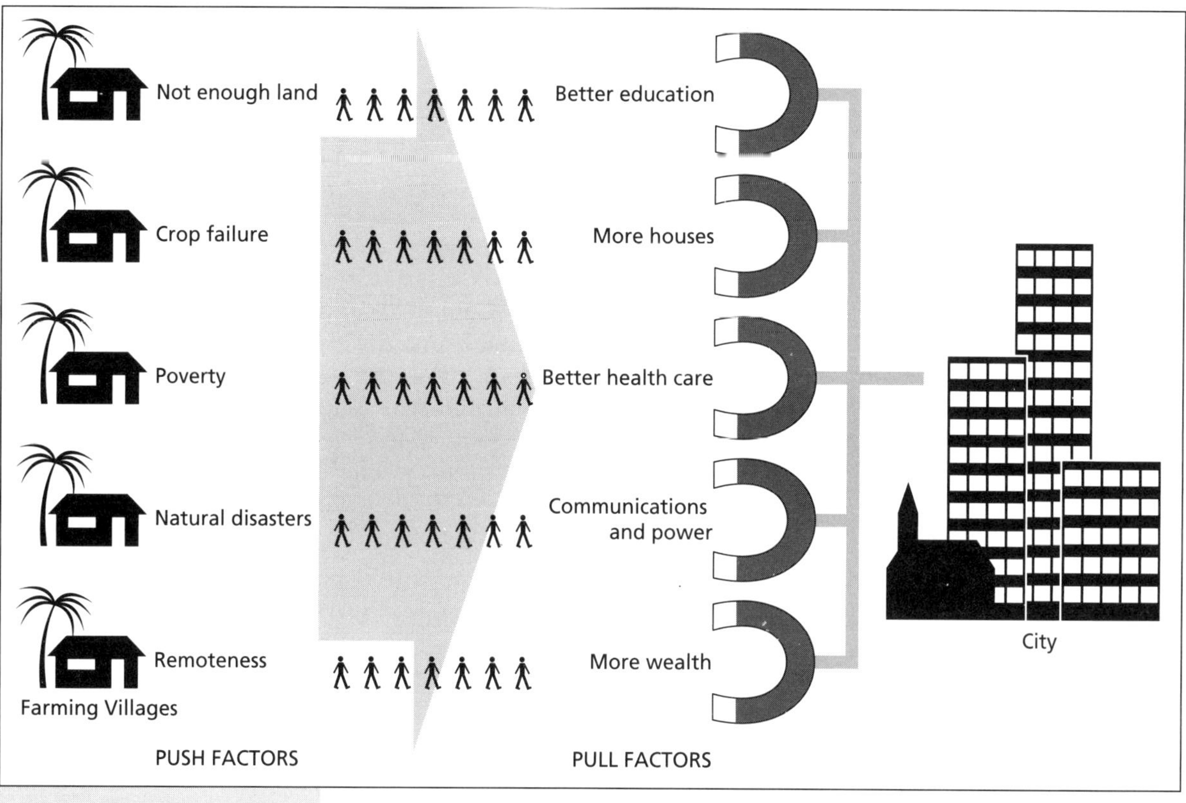

▲ *Figure 1*

Study Figure 1 and complete 1(a). It shows some reasons why people move to cities in LEDCs.

1 a) Name two attractions that encourage people to move to cities. (2 marks)

b) What is rural–urban migration? (2 marks)

2 a) Describe two factors that may encourage people to leave rural areas. (4 marks)

b) Rural areas may become depopulated. Describe two problems caused by depopulation in rural areas. (4 marks)

3 Describe the problems caused by the growth of cities in LEDCs. (6 marks)

4 Urban growth may lead to large areas of shanty towns. Using examples describe the problems people experience living in shanty towns. (6 marks)

5 Using examples, suggest ways in which shanty towns may be improved. (6 marks)

3 Changing city and town centres

How are town and city centres changing in MEDCs?

Key facts

- Competition for land and business pressures have meant changes in land use for retailing, office use, housing and leisure
- People are changing the way they use city centres, where they live and how they travel

The heart of the city is the core and Central Business District which is surrounded by a framework of services and smaller buildings – the inner city. The appearance and use of city centres for retailing, offices, housing and leisure is changing. The use of buildings changes when houses are converted to flats or offices, and warehouses to apartments, tourist sites or small workshops. Land use changes if buildings are demolished and replaced, usually by higher structures.

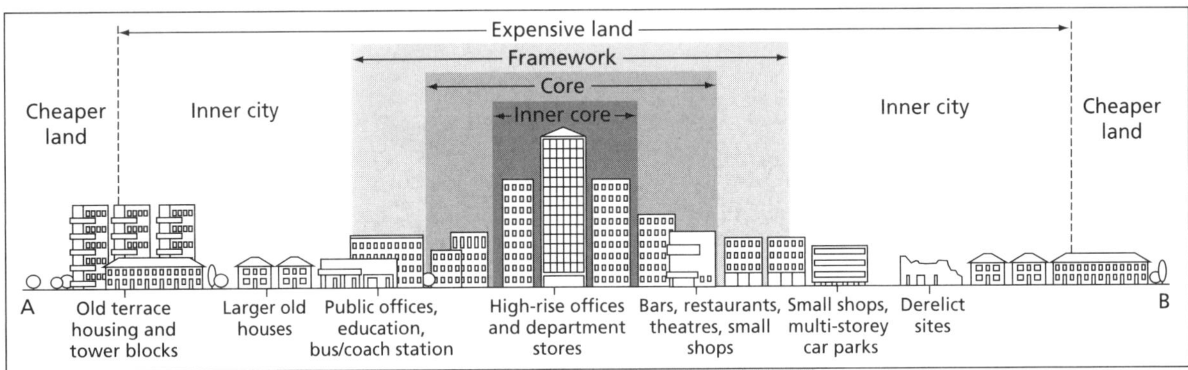

▲ *Cross section of a city centre*

Cities and town centres are changing in many ways:

- Land prices in city centres are increasing as shops, businesses, leisure facilities and services compete for the central, most accessible land. Those who do not want to pay high prices are moving further out to cheaper land.
- People are changing where they live. More wealthy people are moving into central apartments (Manchester census 2002); some are leaving inner-city areas and moving to the suburbs.
- The increased use of cars has had an impact on city centres. Multi-storey car parks surround many central areas of towns and cities, replacing older inner-city housing or industry. Congestion and air pollution have increased.
- Pedestrianized central areas are being created in many city centres.
- People are changing the way they travel in some cities as public transport improves (such as clean, efficient trams in Manchester and Nottingham) and traffic management schemes take effect (such as park and ride facilities and congestion charging).
- People are changing the way they use city centres as facilities and services in major cities are open 24 hours a day.

Definitions

Gentrification Upgrading of houses, which may then become too expensive for local people

Brownfield site A derelict site in an urban area that could be redeveloped (often in inner-city site of older industry)

Greenfield site An agricultural or green site that has not been previously built on

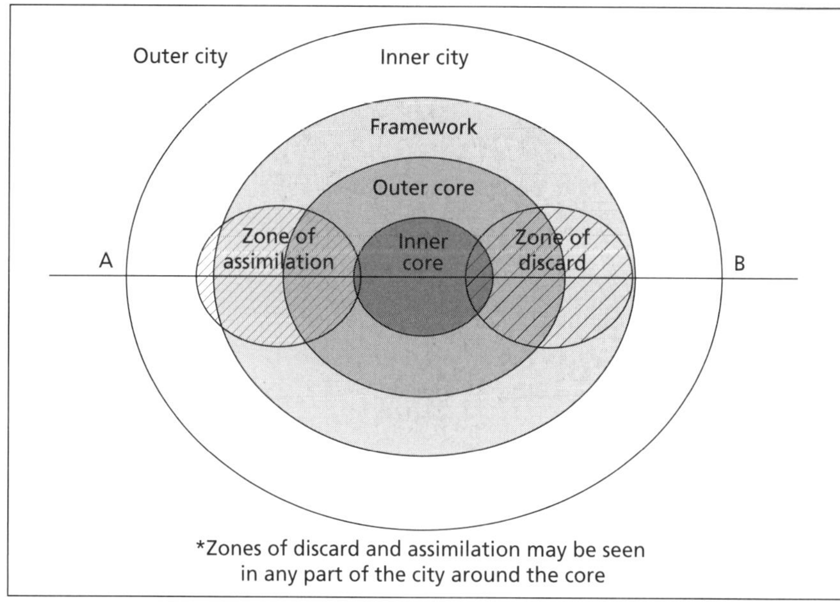

◀ *Land use changes away from the city centre*

Definitions

Zone of assimilation The area of land on the edge of the centre that changes to become part of the CBD

Zone of discard The area in the centre that is no longer needed for city centre functions so becomes run down

The CBD

It may be an area of growth or decline where:

- offices and high buildings are often redeveloped
- there are headquarters of national organizations
- shops, national stores, malls and arcades, perhaps still being developed
- there are pedestrian areas or heavily congested roads with air pollution
- few people live, but some are moving in (e.g. Docklands, London and Manchester)
- there are car parks on brownfield sites on the edge of a CBD, which may be multi-storey for shoppers, business people on redeveloped sites
- there are congested 'through routes' for cars around edge of CBD.

Inner city framework

- Older terrace housing from the nineteenth century may be demolished and replaced with high-rise blocks as in 1970s.
- Poor quality, run-down, unwanted 'slum' areas needing improvement may be gentrified or 'done up' or converted into flats.
- There may be derelict (brownfield) sites needing development.
- Larger older houses may be converted into flats for students or temporary accommodation (perhaps the lowest rents in the area); or converted into smaller offices for insurance companies or estate agents; or gentrified, becoming more expensive housing.

The outer core

- Services such as bus, coach or tram stations and more heavily used roads around the centre.
- Car parks, perhaps on brownfield sites.
- Warehouses converted to offices/heritage sites/flats.
- Education, inner-city primary schools or further education colleges.
- A concentration of bars/clubs/theatres/cinemas/leisure outlets and some housing.

Remember

All cities change. All cities are different. Can you identify change? What should you look for? You can use your local urban area as an example of change in a city or town centre. See how the use of land and buildings has changed. You could make your own mini case study, remembering to be clear about:

1 the location
2 the time span of change (months, years, dates)
3 what was there
4 why things changed
5 what is there now.

You should be able to remember these 5 points in an examination.

What are the problems facing MEDC city centres?

Key facts

- The increasing volumes of traffic cause problems for people who work in, use and live in the city centres.
- Changes in retailing have a big impact on the appearance and use of centres.
- Business needs change so there are problems as land use changes.
- There are environmental problems – congestion, air pollution, dereliction
- The need for high cost, low cost or redeveloped housing creates problems.
- People who live in and use the city may have views about city centre problems that are different to those of planners and developers.

Has retailing change caused problems?

In the 1980s and 1990s city centre stores needing bigger sites and car parking moved to out-of-town retail parks and this has had a big impact on city centres. Some city centre shopping areas declined, shops were left empty and the centre became less attractive (e.g. Dudley, West Midlands, declined when Merry Hill centre was built outside the city).

Shopping malls were built in some cities to improve the centres. There are different problems with malls. They may be busy in the day but when they shut down at night the centre is quiet and empty (like a doughnut with nothing in the middle) and crime and vandalism may become a problem. Malls may be so attractive that other shops in the centre around the mall lose trade. Public streets become private malls and when these malls decline redevelopment is difficult.

What problems are there with housing?

- Some cities have areas of old, decaying housing with social, economic and environmental problems. The quality of life is poor in some parts of Salford, Manchester, for example, where housing is nineteenth-century terraces, with little for children to do and high levels of unemployment. Crime and poverty are big problems. People try to maintain their houses but there is constant vandalism and many want to move out.
- Tower blocks built in the 1970s to replace older housing have been difficult to live in. They are expensive to maintain and may be unattractive homes for people with children or the elderly. Some of the early tower blocks suffered from damp and condensation with lifts that frequently failed.
- There is too little affordable housing especially in some expensive inner cities (e.g. the Manchester centre, and the Docklands, London). Older housing may be replaced, but by apartments or houses that are too expensive for the people who originally lived there. Many cities now have a shortage of low-cost housing for people who work in the cities and cannot afford to commute long distances from the suburbs.

What problems are caused by traffic in cities?

Traffic, particularly cars, cause problems when moving (congestion, pollution etc) and when stationary (parking for shopping, for residents).

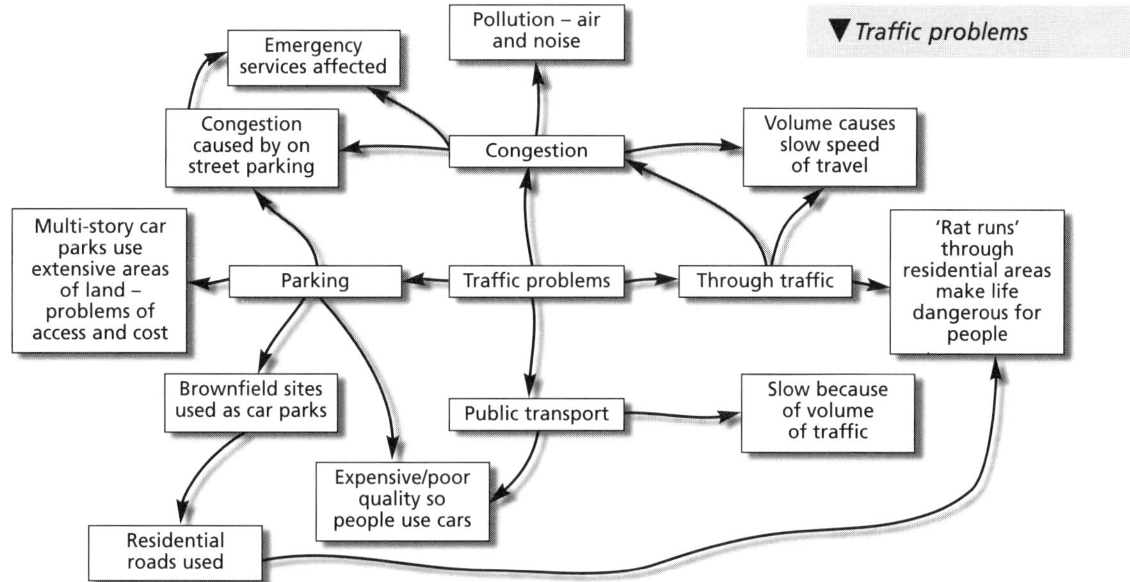

▼ *Traffic problems*

What about other land use changes?

- The decline in manufacturing leaves empty factories and derelict land.
- Some offices are moving away from the expensive city centres, leaving empty buildings and fewer jobs. Some businesses are moving into the city and replacing housing, shops etc.
- The increase in pubs, clubs and leisure places brings in lots of people and money but it can increase crime and vandalism, particularly at night.
- Areas of land use change on the edges of the CBD (zones of discard) and are often derelict and unattractive environments.
- Brownfield sites (old industrial or housing sites) are areas of decay until cleaned up and redeveloped.
- If areas on the edge of the CBD become attractive for developers (zones of assimilation) rents may go up and residents or businesses already there who cannot afford the new rents may be displaced.

Remember

You may be living in an area with traffic congestion, poor housing or derelict sites. Redevelopment may have caused other problems which affect you or other age groups, young or old. Work out the following five points to add to your revision notes.

1 Make sure that you know what the problem is.

2 Who it is a problem for (gentrification is not a problem for the people who now live in the houses but it is a problem for the people who used to live in the area and can no longer afford to do so).

3 Find out how long the problem has existed.

4 Why the problem has occurred.

5 Try to decide how the problems link together, e.g. does traffic congestion affect the way people shop; does the decline of one industry lead to the decline of a whole area?

Try to briefly note some facts and figures so that you have details to use in the examination answer and you do not write generally about somewhere you know well.

How can MEDC cities be managed and improved?

Managing city centres in the UK

Managing housing
Much housing has been improved and many new homes have been built in regeneration schemes (e.g. Docklands, London). Tower blocks have been improved or demolished in many cities (e.g. Nightingale Estate, Hackney, London). Security systems and upgraded facilities improve the quality of life for residents. Residents' associations, neighbourhood watch and other self-help schemes enable people to improve the quality of their own lives, but lack of money is one of the biggest problems for individuals and authorities.

Urban regeneration
Schemes improve the area and social problems by addressing environmental decay, poor housing, brownfield sites and pollution. Jobs and money are attracted to the area. The most successful schemes involve local people as in Glasgow, Manchester or Birmingham.

Managing retail change
Redevelopment of town and city centres around new retail sites and pedestrianized areas has helped to keep the cities busy and prosperous. Big shopping malls and pedestrian areas have been built in places as different as Southampton (in 2000), Manchester (from 1997) and Basingstoke (in 2002). Smaller towns (such as Taunton) have made the town centre more attractive to shoppers.

Managing transport
Many ideas are being tried. Car use is being discouraged by congestion charging (e.g. Durham, 2002), high parking charges, reduced speed limits and one way systems. Public transport use is being encouraged. Trams, better buses, light railways, low fares, bus lanes to make public transport travel faster and new systems developed (e.g. Metrolink, Manchester). Traffic is managed on roads with bus lanes, cycle routes, car sharing, computerized traffic lights, traffic calming etc.

Are there problems with the solutions?
Every city centre management scheme will have advantages and disadvantages; some people will be pleased, others will not. Priority bus lanes will please public transport users but not the people in cars in traffic jams. Houses and businesses may be displaced by big regeneration schemes. Pubs and clubs bring life back to the city centre at night but also bring problems of crime and vandalism.

Case study

Manchester and urban regeneration

Bomb damage in 1996 prompted regeneration of the city centre. The heart of the city was replanned and rebuilt rather than repaired. The city is an important international centre as well as a regional centre and tourism is an important factor in its regeneration.

The centre now has:

- 'state of the art stores' in a retail and commercial core
- a Millenium Quarter around the Cathedral with a square, a city park, visitor centre and Urbis – a visitor attraction and cultural facility
- new squares and a pedestrian friendly environment
- a futuristic leisure complex
- a traffic-free centre, inner relief road to take traffic, a Metrolink tram service
- more people living in the centre (10 000 in 2001 and only 1000 in 1991), many in redeveloped industrial buildings.

▲ *New Manchester*

The centre of Manchester is thriving but some people will see disadvantages in such a big change. Some people will say that the run-down inner-city areas nearby were in greater need of help.

Case study

Traffic management in London

The average speed of travel across London may now be only 2.7 mph. Congestion charging (in 2003) is one way of reducing the number of cars on the roads. There are many disadvantages for local people who live on the charge boundary line who may have to pay to take children to school, go to church etc. Some roads just outside the charge zone become very busy as people try to avoid crossing the line. Communities are divided. The quality of life for local people decreases in order to improve the quality of life for the majority.

Congestion charging...

WHAT is it?
The £5 daily congestion charge ... raising millions each week to be re-invested in the transport system.

WHERE is it?
The congestion charging zone covers central London.

WHEN is it?
From 17 February 2003.

BusPlus

Making your bus service better

The **BusPlus** programme is a new £200 million initiative designed to make a real difference to the quality of some of London's key bus routes.

Over the next three years, 70 key bus routes across London will be upgraded to make them more reliable, safer, cleaner and more comfortable than ever before.

Remember

Keep track of what is happening in your nearest city or town; every urban centre has traffic problems.

You should know:

1 What schemes are taking place
2 Who is affected
3 The advantages and disadvantages of schemes
4 What people hope the scheme will achieve or has achieved
5 Why you think it is successful or unsuccessful.

Making the grade

Using the Internet

You can use the Internet in two ways:

- to find extra material and information to add to your existing 'notes'
- to use revision sites to help you revise.

Finding extra material

- Search, using key words from the specification, to try to make sure that you focus on the correct aspects. You should be thinking about issues.
- The order in which you put the search words is important. If you want to find out more about hurricanes and you use the search word 'hurricanes' you will find some complicated, scientific sites that look as if they have a lot of data, if you could find it. It is also tempting to click on something that looks familiar like 'what to do in a hurricane' which is not really relevant. 'Hurricane Mitch' as a search will bring you all sorts of useful data. 'Mitch' without the hurricane will find some very different themes.
- If you are sifting through a number of potential sites, think about the detail you need and the issues involved. For example, global warming should be researched in relation to global economic development, the problems and issues, so try a pressure group website. Long articles and lists of facts are not a great help to you and using just the search word 'global warming' will find pages and pages of facts.
- Do not print a page of information and think that you have revised! Try to select 5–10 brief pieces of information that support your existing work and that you will be able to remember.
- Build up a small file of useful data and organize it into sections that match your specification.
- Print information with the web address, because if you do not, you will probably want to find more information at a later date and you will not remember where to find the site.
- Can you use your local area? Try 'glass recycling' in your local authority A–Z website as well as in a wider search. Try to think about the detail you would like to find from a local authority and if the A–Z is not easy to use try being specific, e.g. 'Manchester regeneration Ancoats'.

Using revision sites

- Revision sites can be useful but they are not designed to fit particular specifications. So you need to select the appropriate sections. Some revision sections may provide data for more than one question in the examination.
- They will enable you to revise some things in a different way.
- They may be useful if you have missed a particular section at school or if you want to go back to the basics in looking at key stage 3 data.
- Do know what you are looking for – your specification.
- Do remember that you are thinking about issues.
- Do persevere in looking through a site but do not think that revision sites will solve all your problems.
- A revision site is only as good as your selection!

Websites

Many revision sites can be found to cover basic material to be used with all geography specifications.

Others provide a huge amount of UK data and other sources will give you information that may be useful if you search with – 'geography GCSE revision key stage 4'. But you need to be very selective. Go to www.heinemann.co.uk/hotlinks and insert code 9957P to access some very useful geography revision resources.

Revision sites can be very useful but very time consuming and they may be most useful towards the end of the revision time when you have checked through all your own data. Only use them if you know lots already and you know what you are looking for!

Exam practice questions

Study Figure 1, the sketch map of some urban planning schemes in Greater Manchester.

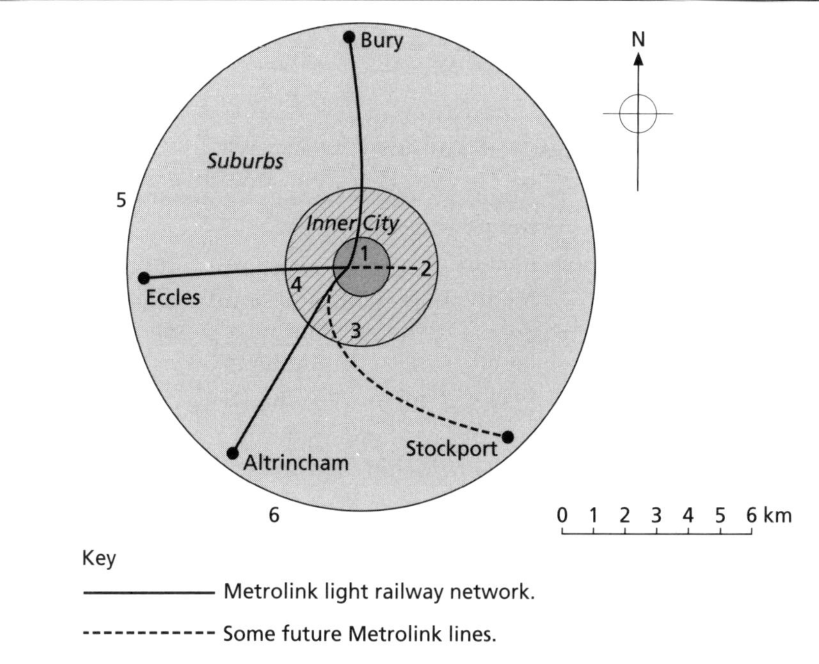

1 CBD (re-development of sites affected by 1996 bomb damage).
2 Site of new stadium for the Commonwealth Games 2002.
3 Hulme – rebuilt inner city housing area, replacing 1960's high-rise blocks with smaller scale property designed in consultation with local people.
4 Salford Quays – former dockland area with high quality private housing and the new "Lowry" arts centre.
5 Trafford centre – an out-of-town shopping centre.
6 Manchester Airport – second runway development.

▲ *Figure 1*

1 **a)** Give an example of an urban planning scheme in the inner city. (1 mark)

b) Give one reason for change in the inner city. (1 mark)

c) Suggest three problems local people in Hulme may have experienced before housing was rebuilt. (6 marks)

2 Using examples you have studied, describe the problems caused by the decline of inner cities in a More Economically Developed Country (MEDC)) such as the United Kingdom. (6 marks)

3 Suggest ways in which pedestrianization and public transport may be used to manage change in MEDC cities. (6 marks)

4 Choose one example of an urban planning scheme you have studied. Describe the scheme and explain whether it has met people's needs. (6 marks)

4 Pressure at the rural–urban fringe

How is land use changing at the rural–urban fringe?

Key facts

- The rural–urban fringe lies between the built-up urban area and open countryside.
- Within it there may be woodland, fields, housing estates, retail parks, a golf course, trading estates, or a business park.
- Developments such as new housing estates contribute to urban sprawl and the expansion of the rural–urban fringe.

How have cars contributed to land use change?

More people use cars now than ever before. The average commuting distance of 13 km reflects the increase in the number of people who travel across the rural–urban fringe to work. Industrial and leisure developments in the rural–urban fringe or near motorway junctions attract more people and more cars and often more housing.

Definitions

Counter urbanization People moving from urban areas to rural areas or small towns.
Suburbanization of villages An increase in house building and development around villages or around towns near to the villages that makes the village like a suburb.
A pressure group A group of people who join together to make their views known, usually about an issue. They can be either a proactive group, which exists all the time (e.g. Friends of the Earth, a permanent international pressure group) or a reactive group. The latter is set up as a result of a particular event (e.g. a local group set up in response to a new road or development which may only last only a few months).
NGO (Non Governmental Organization) An organization that concerns itself with issues but is neither funded nor controlled by a national government (e.g. Oxfam and World Wildlife Fund).

How is housing changing?

- About 100 000 people in the UK move to the countryside every year.
- In 1998 the Government estimated that 4.3 million more homes were needed (due to more people living on their own, people living longer, smaller family units).
- Many of the people who move out of the suburbs are families, retired or wealthy and they are looking for housing with space and gardens.
- The greatest growth of housing in the UK is in the South East and in the rural–urban fringe. Housing developments vary in size from 2 or 3 houses to large estates (e.g. Bluewater development in Kent has attracted planned development of 20 000 houses).

What has happened to retailing?

The majority of people use cars to shop so large and small retail complexes with good road or motorway access have been built near urban areas (e.g. Bluewater, Kent). Most towns/cities have a store in the rural–urban fringe so out-of-town retail floor space has grown from 0.3 million metres in 1975 to 5.8 million sq metres in 2000. Further big shop development in the rural–urban fringe will not now take place but growth is still taking place around existing ones.

Are there changes in the rural–urban fringe land use in leisure?

- Leisure centres, cinemas, hotel and catering facilities are built in the rural–urban fringe (due to cheaper land, good road access, parking).
- Some rural–urban fringe land has changed from farming to riding, golf courses, woodland, fishing, farm museum/shop etc. Most people use cars to get to these activities.

How is industry changing?

- Industries and trading estates have developed in the rural–urban fringe because of good access (motorways and roads) and big sites/cheap land (e.g. the M4 junctions, Bristol).
- Many fringe industries are 'footloose' (i.e. not tied to a raw material location) and so may locate in the rural–urban fringe because of good housing, attractive countryside, good road access, cheap land.
- Hi-tech industries may follow a motorway between urban areas (e.g. along the M4) or locate in attractive areas.
- Science and business parks are attracted to the rural–urban fringe (e.g. Cambridge). Road access, the environment, costs, etc. are better than in city centres.

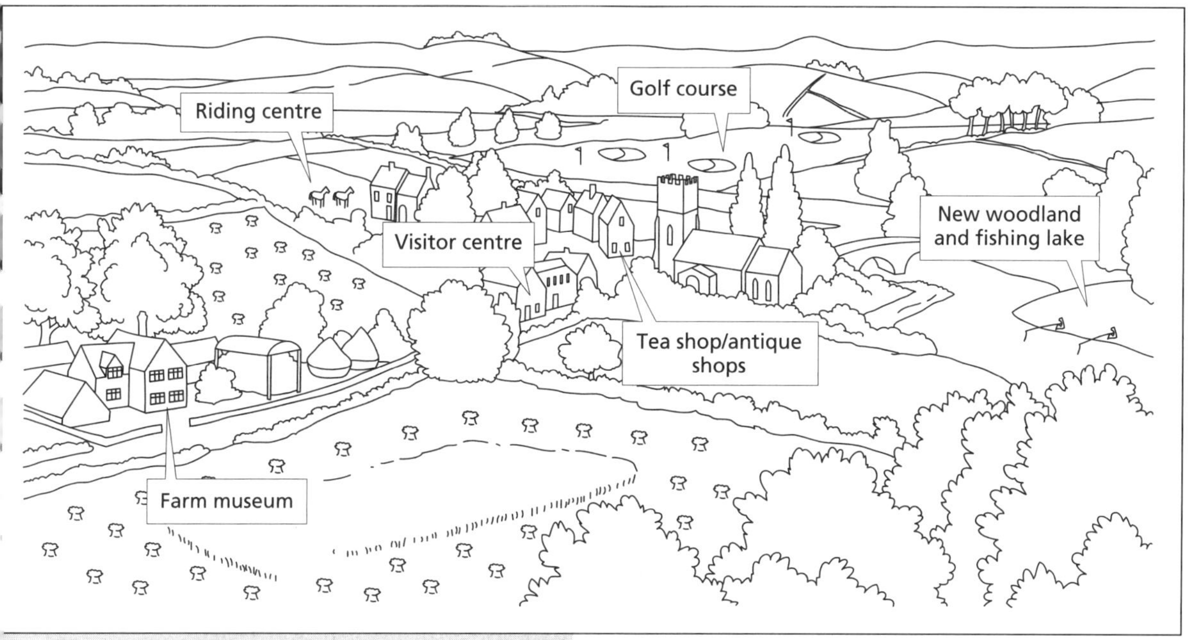

▲ *Some uses of green belt land*

What are the 'push' factors from the city?

High land and building costs, congestion, slow travel time, noise, pollution, crime, lack of green space, expensive housing.

What are the 'pull' factors to the country?

Cheap land, good road access, space, quiet, good quality of life, cheaper/bigger/better housing.

Remember

Your best source of information may be around you if you live near the rural–urban fringe. Try to identify five points to illustrate change.

1. Look for changes in land use for housing, industry, leisure and retail and decide on the one you will investigate.
2. Find out how the land is used now, the extent of the area.
3. What was there before?
4. What have been the effects of the change on the area on roads, access, volume of traffic, people using the site, jobs etc.
5. How has it affected the local people and the environment? Look for positives and negatives.

What are the impacts of changing land use at the rural–urban fringe?

The impacts of change at the rural–urban fringe are felt in the countryside and the city and both areas are affected by increased traffic through commuting.

Key facts

- Countryside is lost to buildings (trading estates), roads or green leisure (golf).
- Employment increases (plus commuting), particularly in service industries (retailing, leisure, distribution).
- Facilities used by rural and urban people increase (retail park, cinema, DIY store).
- The neighbouring CBD may be negatively affected, and decline.
- Government, local authorities and pressure groups such as Friends of the Earth may be in conflict over land use change and development.

Definitions

Urban growth The expansion in towns and cities
Urban sprawl The spread of cities into the rural area extending the rural–urban fringe
Conurbation Several urban areas merge reducing the rural–urban fringe

What are the negative effects of development at the rural–urban fringe?

- Countryside is lost to all sorts of building (usually low rise) such as retail parks, cinemas, industry, warehouses and housing.
- Housing estates may change the character of life in the rural–urban fringe.
- Roads may become congested as people commute to work or drive out to the new developments. Traffic creates air and noise pollution.
- Leisure use of the countryside such as golf and riding changes the environment, as does a type of leisure farming rather than commercial farming.

What are the advantages of development?

- Employment is created (shops, services, transport, building etc).
- New roads can make travel through the rural–urban fringe easier and faster.
- Facilities are easy to get to for people in the rural areas and for people in the urban areas
- A better lifestyle is possible in homes with space, gardens, clean air and parking.
- Housing can be built easily and cheaply on greenfield sites.

Who decides whether the impact of development is good or bad?

A development that is good for some people may have negative effects on others. Some developments benefit people who live somewhere else.

Case study

Plans for expansion at Stansted Airport

The Government has proposed building up to three new runways at Stansted airport, Essex. Plans were opposed in October 2002 by groups of people who considered that their lives would be adversely affected. 'Stop Stansted Expansion Group' has led protests. Hertfordshire County Council expressed 'grave concern over the government's threatened attack on Hertfordshire's environment' and the quality of life of its residents with 'increased noise, traffic, pollution and urbanization' (2 November 2002). Affected villages and towns as well as the National Trust also disagree with the proposal.

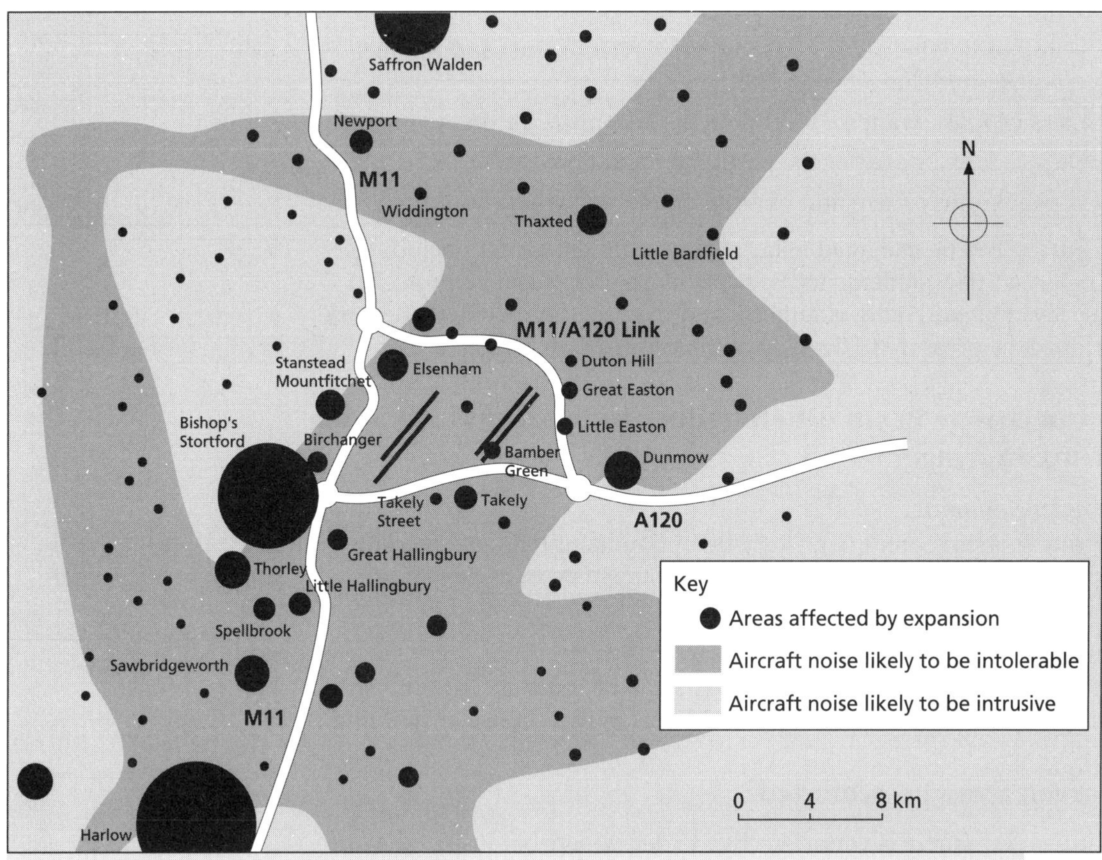

▲ *Stansted airport and proposed expansion. The map shows the urban and rural–urban fringe areas affected by the new road (M11/A120) and runways (e.g. Bishop's Stortford).*

People who opposed the plans estimated that the expansion of Stansted would have an adverse impact on the health and well being of 600 000 people and result in the loss of countryside and heritage sites. They estimated that 83 000 people in 70 towns and villages would have 'intolerable' noise and 65 million people will travel to the airport. More housing (as in Bishop's Stortford, 2 miles from Stansted) would be needed for the people who would work there.

However, millions of travellers would benefit and thousands of jobs would be created (bringing money to the area) and housing.

Remember

There may be opposition to a housing or other development in your area. Find out the size and extent of the development.

1. How it would change the area?
2. What the purpose of the development is, so who would benefit?
3. What would be lost? Who would lose?
4. Would the development help people in the local or a wider area?

How can pressure at the rural–urban fringe be managed?

Who has a voice in how rural–urban fringe areas are managed?

Many groups of people are involved in managing the changes and conflicts in the rural–urban fringe.

- Government – makes planning regulations and requires the building of more houses
- Local authority – manages planning and developments and follows government guidelines
- Business people – want to develop in the best place for them
- NGOs – such as Friends of the Earth have a national view
- Local people – live there and have an opinion on what should happen.

Urban sprawl can be managed using several different tactics, including green belts and new settlements. Special environments can be protected through law. In cities, redevelopments and the use of brownfield sites can help reduce the pressure to develop at the rural–urban fringe.

How can change in cities help reduce pressure on land at the rural–urban fringe?

CBD redevelopment
Major new shopping areas (e.g. West Quay, Southampton) and housing developments (e.g. Docklands, London) encourage people to use city centres, though congestion may increase.

Brownfield sites
Sites previously used for industry/housing can be redeveloped but cleaning sites is expensive and adds to the cost of each house or building.

Can green areas be protected?

The rural–urban fringe is very attractive to developers because of the greater space available so green areas need to be protected from extensive building. Planners in the local authority can refuse development in some rural areas that they decide need preserving but the Government can over-rule them if they decide the development (usually housing) is more important than the conservation need. Independent groups such as the National Trust may help to preserve green land they consider to be 'of natural beauty' and local groups will campaign to prevent developments they consider damaging.

Areas can be designated as SSSIs, sites of special scientific interest, when special habitats are threatened by development but, even if protected, they may change as building spreads around them. One such area is Canford Heath, to the west of the rapidly expanding urban area of Bournemouth and Poole where housing spreads into open country. Canford Heath is one of the largest heathlands in the UK that is not a nature reserve. It is a conservation area with rare reptiles, sand lizards and smooth snakes. Housing has been built on some parts of the Heath and the reptiles were moved to other preserved areas.

Can urban sprawl be managed?

Green belts

Bands of farmland/green land can be preserved around a city to prevent urban sprawl and maintain an attractive environment. The first Green Belt Act was in 1938. There are, however, some disadvantages:

- Development has jumped the green belt so commuting increases.
- Roads/motorways have been built which attract industry.
- Redundant farm buildings are being converted to other uses.
- Pressure on city land increases because the city cannot grow outwards.

New towns

There are 33 new towns in the UK, home to about 1.3 million people. After the New Town Act of 1946 a ring of towns were built around London (including Stevenage, Harlow and Bracknell) to provide accommodation for people from London and prevent urban sprawl. Others were built near major urban centres. Work, housing and leisure would all be in one place so that people could have a good quality of life with access to the countryside. When work became unavailable people started commuting to other urban areas, crossing greenbelts and increasing congestion. Some new town centres are being redeveloped now (e.g. Bracknell) 50 years after they were built. New towns were built in other countries (including Egypt, Malaysia and France). Marne-la-Vallée, east of Paris has grown to 250 000 people since the 1960s and includes Disneyland. This is one of several new towns around Paris.

Case study

Bracknell as a new town

Bracknell was one of the first eight new towns designated to accommodate people from central London. The population was planned as 25 000 growing around a small market town of 5000 and the first 50 houses were finished in 1950. Bracknell Development Corporation was set up to build a self-contained town combining town life with the advantages of the country and planned on the neighbourhood principle, with a group of shops, a primary school, a church, a community centre and a public house in each area. Nine original neighbourhoods housed from 3000 to 9000 people, all landscaped to retain open space and trees. Many firms moved to the town and throughout the 1970s and 1980s Bracknell grew in employment, housing population and facilities. The town centre was redeveloped and pedestrianized in the 1960s but further redevelopment from 2002 will see 'a major new town centre'. The town is now the unitary authority of Bracknell Forest with a population in 2001 of nearly 110 000 but it is still advertised as 'set in beautiful Berkshire countryside' combining 'country villages with the bustle of a big town and an enviable quality of life.' Bracknell's growth may have produced its own problems of rural–urban fringe management.

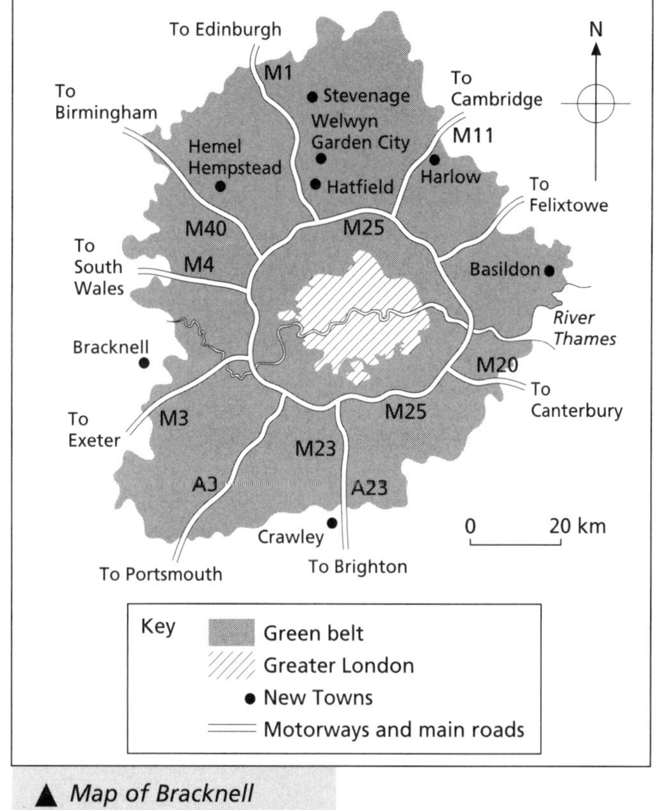

▲ *Map of Bracknell*

Making the grade

Using your local area

You can use your local area as relevant case study material for some of the exam questions but can you make the best use of your knowledge? Do you know the details that will give you access to the higher level marks? 'There is a leisure centre outside town' is not enough! You need the location, name, who uses it, how people get there, and what the problems are.

Can you be prepared?

- Look at what is around you and think names, locations and details.
- What has changed, what is changing? Who has been affected by the changes? Are there environmental, economic or social gains or losses?
- Who lives there? Who uses the area? Who makes decisions about what happens?
- Where can you find information? Look for your local authority website which should have details of what is happening and what is planned. The local paper may have information about issues.
- In which sections of the specification could you use your own area?
- Has the population changed? Make use of the 2001 UK census.
- Has the land use changed? Is there a retail park near you? Has the town or city centre changed or has a nearby city centre changed?
- What pressures are there on the physical environment (coastal erosion, tourism)?
- What weather hazards are there (think floods, storms)?
- What changes have there been in the levels of development (quality of life and development in your area)?
- Is resource depletion an issue (think mining, energy production, alternative energy supplies, recycling, resource use)?
- How is economic development being managed (think global problems locally, acid rain, global warming and sea level rise, storms, pollution)?
- Is tourism an issue (local tourism and changing patterns of tourism)? How does it effect the local economy?
- Do give a picture of the situation or issue in your local area that somebody from outside the area would understand.

Remember

Case studies from your local area can be just as useful as one from another area (unless you are answering a question on an LEDC!)

To help you revise use a word map. Build on it by thinking of how change (in local population growth) affects housing, roads, and villages. What are the problems and benefits? Are there links? Can you see how change in one part might affect another?

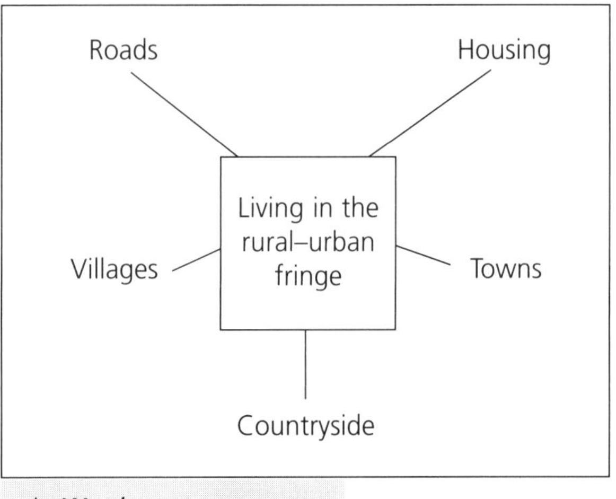

▲ *Word map*

Exam practice questions

Study Figure 1 and complete 1(a) and (b).

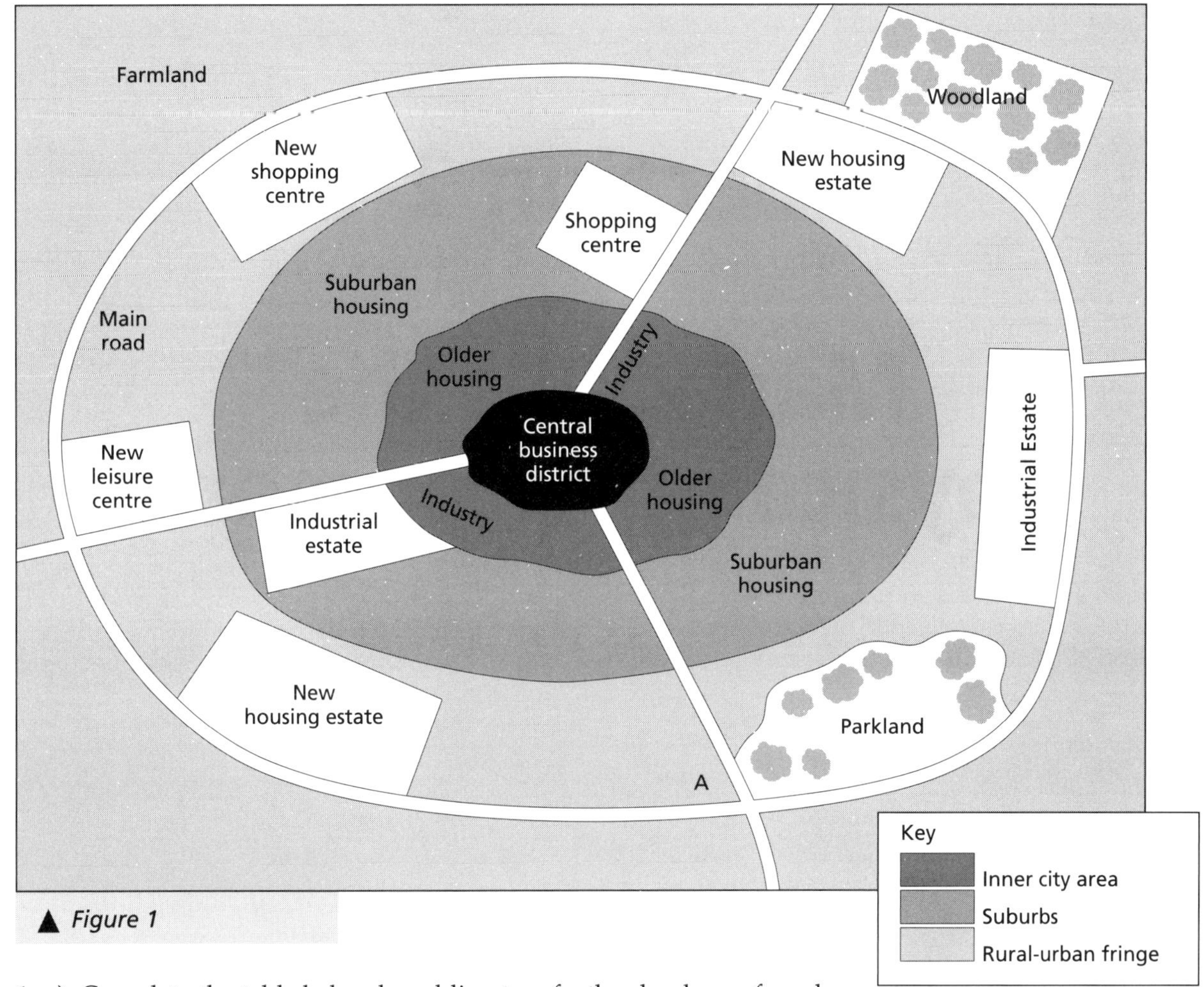

▲ *Figure 1*

1 a) Complete the table below by adding two further land uses found in the rural–urban fringe.

Land use in rural–urban fringe:
New shopping centre
New housing estate

b) A golf course is planned at location A on Figure 1. Suggest two reasons why this could be a good location. (2 marks)

c) Suggest the disadvantages of building in the rural–urban fringe. (2 marks)

2 Why are new housing estates often found in the rural–urban fringe? (4 marks)

3 Suggest reasons why the redevelopment of an inner city may reduce development in the rural–urban fringe. (6 marks)

4 Explain why the development of the rural–urban fringe may cause conflict. (6 marks)

Section 2

Managing the physical environment

Revision checklist

Use this page to check that you have covered everything you need to. If you can't answer any of the questions, go back to the relevant section.

5 Living with tectonic hazards	• Where are earthquakes and volcanoes found? • What are the causes and features of tectonic activity? • Why do people choose to live near tectonic hazards? • Why do the effects of tectonic hazards vary between countries? • How can the risks and effects of tectonic activity be reduced? • Why are aid agencies important to LEDCs after a natural disaster?
6 Weather hazards	• What are tropical storms like and how do they develop? • What natural and human factors help to cause flooding? • What are the primary effects of storms and flooding? • What are the secondary effects of storms and flooding? • How can the risks and effects of storms be reduced? • How can the risk and effects of flooding be reduced?
7 Water and food supply	• Which parts of the world have poor supplies of water and food? • What natural and human factors help to create water and food problems? • What is desertification and how is it caused? • What are the impacts of poor water and food supplies on human life? • How can the availability of food and water be increased? • What part can aid agencies play in improving water and food supplies?
8 Pressures on the physical environment	• What part does weathering, erosion, transportation and deposition play in the formation of natural environments? • Why has the number of people visiting National Parks increased? • What is a 'honeypot' site and why are they popular? • What are the economic and environmental effects of tourism in National Parks? • What strategies can be used to manage National Parks and honeypot sites? • What are the advantages and disadvantages of management strategies?

5 Living with tectonic hazards

Why are earthquakes and volcanoes found in particular places?

What are tectonic plates?

The Earth's crust is divided into large blocks called plates. The heat inside the Earth creates currents which move the plates around.

- Oceanic plates carry the oceans.
- Continental plates carry the continents.

What happens where plates meet?

The places where plates meet are called plate margins or boundaries. It is often in these places that the Earth is unstable resulting in earthquakes and volcanoes.

What are the different types of plate margins (boundaries)?

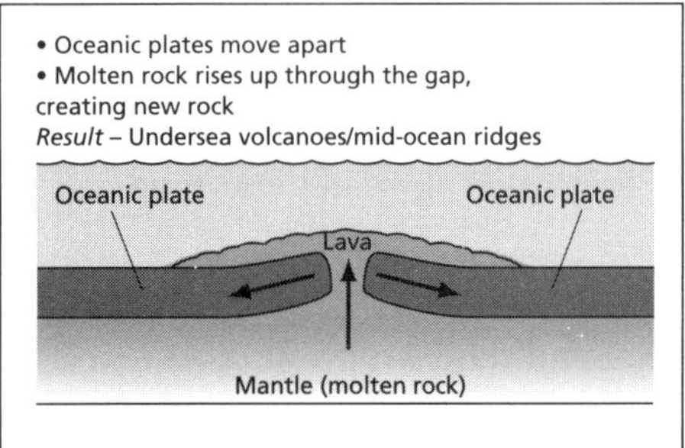

▲ *A constructive margin*

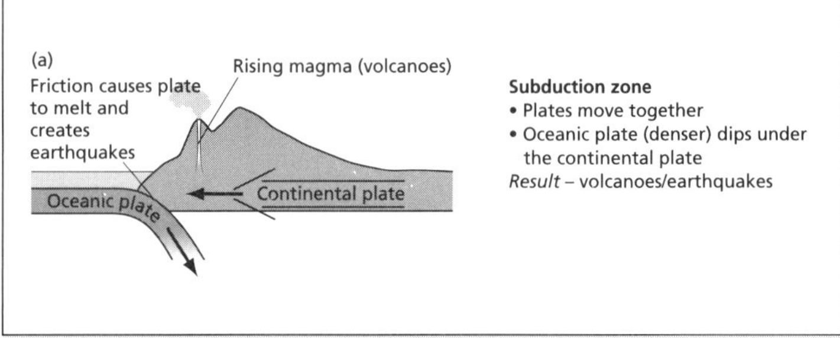

▲ *(a) A destructive margin: a subduction zone*

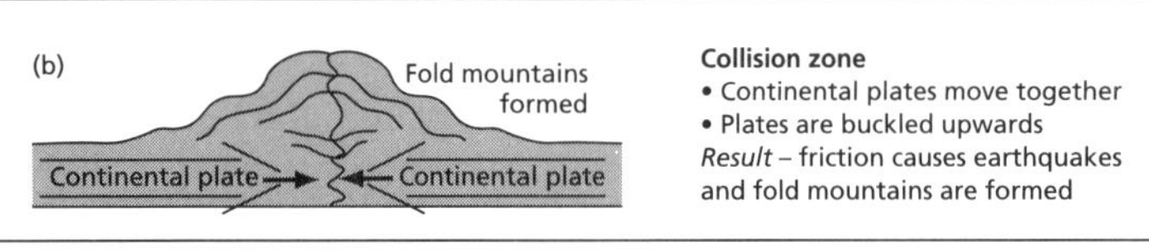

◀ *(b) A destructive margin: a collision zone*

How fast do plates move?

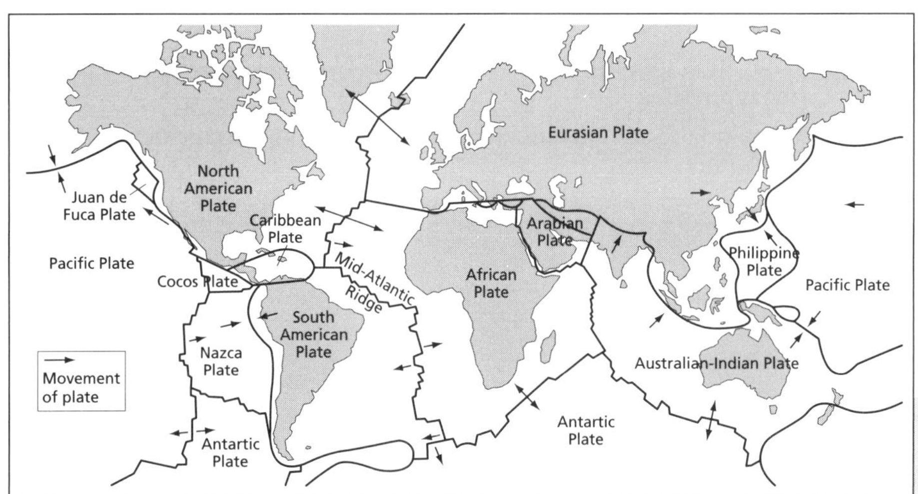

◀ *The Earth's major plates and plate boundaries*

The rate of movement varies, but in general it is between 2 and 12 cm a year. Over thousands of years this can make a big difference to the Earth's surface.

What are earthquakes?

Earthquakes occur where plates are moving towards or alongside each other (e.g. the conservative plate margin at the San Andreas Fault in California, USA). Pressure builds up until there is a sudden movement, sending a shockwave through the Earth's crust.

How are earthquakes measured?

- The vibrations during an earthquake are measured using a seismometer. This produces a seismograph.
- The Meralli scale measures the amount of shaking.
- The Richter scale measures the energy released, on a scale of 1 to 10.

What are volcanoes?

Volcanoes are formed when semi-molten rock (magma) rises to the Earth's surface. When the magma reaches the Earth's surface it becomes lava.

Key fact

The movement of the Earth's plates is called plate tectonics.

Definitions – earthquakes

Focus The point where the shockwave starts
Epicentre The point above the focus on the Earth's surface

Key facts

- The Earth's crust is divided into plates.
- A plate margin or boundary is where plates meet.
- Most tectonic activity (earthquakes/volcanoes) occurs close to plate margins.
- Earthquakes are caused when plates stick together and continued pressure causes sudden movement.
- Volcanoes occur where magma rises to the surface through cracks in the Earth's crust.

What are the different types of volcano?

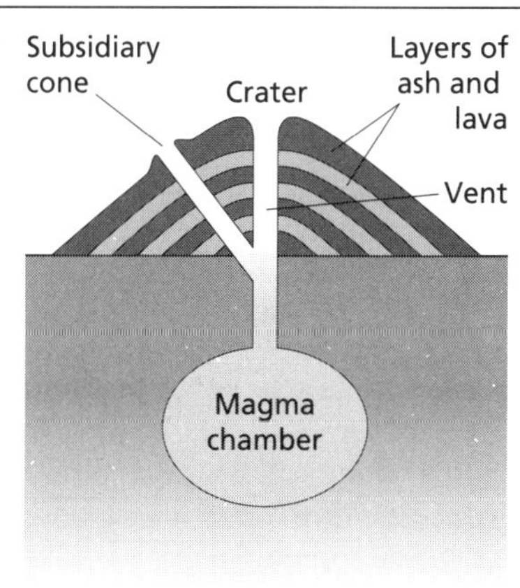

(a) **Composite volcano**
Example: Mount St Helens, USA
Characteristics:
- Steep-sided cone
- Alternate layers of acid lava and ash
- Lava may cool inside the vent – the next eruption is very explosive to remove the plug
- Subsidiary cones and vents form

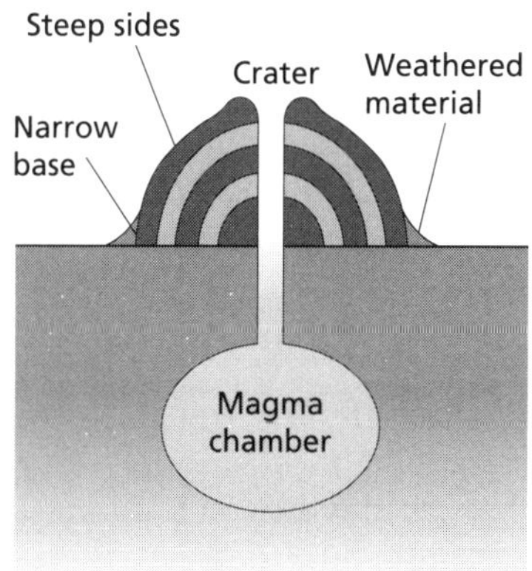

(b) **Acid lava volcano**
Example: Mont Pelee, Martinique
Characteristics:
- Very steep cone with narrow base
- Composed of acid lava which does not flow easily
- Very explosive eruptions: Mont Pelee erupted very violently in 1902. The clouds of ash and lava killed 30 000 people

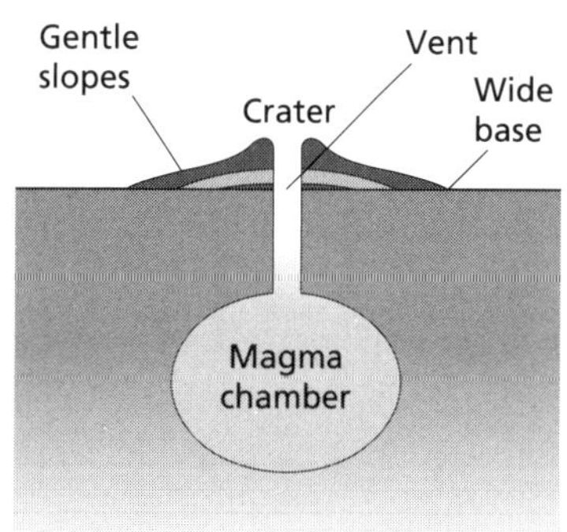

(c) **Shield volcano** (basic lava)
Example: Mauna Loa on the Hawaiian Islands
Characteristics:
- Gentle slopes and wide base
- Frequent eruptions of basic lava
- Lava flows more easily, travels longer distances before cooling
- Usually non-violent

▲ *Types of volcanoes*

Why do the effects of tectonic hazards vary?

Tectonic activity (earthquakes and volcanoes) occurs around the world but often goes unnoticed if no-one lives in the area affected. It is only when people are involved that it becomes a hazard – usually the more built-up the area the greater the hazard.

The effects of tectonic hazards vary because:

- some places are nearer to the source of earthquakes or volcanoes
- some places are better prepared than others
- some places have more resources to deal with the effects of the hazard.

There are other factors, such as the time of day that the hazard occurred and how powerful it was.

Key facts

Primary effects

Immediate effects of a natural disaster:

- Death/injury
- Loss of land/buildings
- Damage to infrastructure

Secondary effects

Longer term effects of a natural disaster:

- Lack of shelter
- Poor water/food supply
- Loss of income
- Long-term damage to infrastructure

Case study

MEDC

The Kobe earthquake, Japan, 1995

When?

- The earthquake struck at 5.46am on 17 January 1995.

Where and how?

- The epicentre was in Osaka Bay.
- The earthquake measured 7.2 on the Richter scale.
- The nearby port of Kobe was badly affected.
- The nearby business centres of the cities Osaka and Kyoto suffered significant damage.

Primary effects:

- 5 477 people were killed.
- 316 000 people were made homeless.
- 12 trains were derailed.
- Part of the elevated Hanshin Expressway collapsed.
- The port facilities were destroyed.
- Water and gas mains ruptured cutting off supply to one million homes.

Secondary effects:

- Fires spread as a result of ruptured gas mains.
- Thousands of businesses were forced to close.
- Trade in and out of the port was seriously affected.

What help was given?

- 316 000 people were given emergency accommodation.
- Meals and bottled water were flown in.
- The Japanese army co-ordinated rescue efforts.

Rebuilding the area

- Buildings were reconstructed using stronger frames.
- Roads and railways were repaired or rebuilt.
- Thousands of new buildings were constructed.

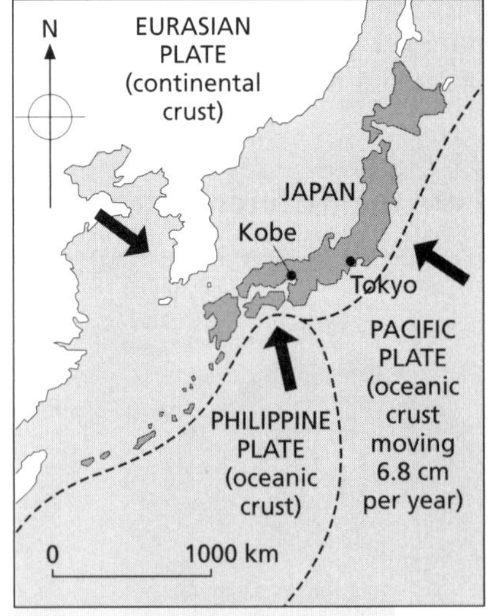

▲ *The Kobe earthquake*

Remember

You may be asked to compare the impacts of hazards between MEDCs and LEDCs.

Case study

The Gujarat earthquake, India, 2001

LEDC

People in Gujarat state are trying to rebuild their lives after India's worst earthquake in almost 50 years. The earthquake struck on 26 January 2001 and measured 7.9 on the Richter scale. Further aftershocks added to the devastation. Twenty thousand people are thought to have died, but the full death toll may never be known as thousands more may have been buried beneath the rubble.

After the earthquake, people helped International rescue teams to dig through the debris in search of survivors and the Indian government used extra aircraft to fly some of the injured to other urban centres such as Mumbai (Bombay). Emergency services were at breaking point in their attempts to cope with the thousands of injured, and to provide food, water and clothing for the half a million homeless, who had to bear baking temperatures during the day and bitterly cold temperatures sleeping out at night. Worst hit was the city of Bhuj, located near the epicentre of the earthquake. Whole villages surrounding the city were flattened.

Three months after the earthquake:

- Estimated 30 000 dead
- Estimated 150 000 injured
- 1 million still homeless
- Many unstable buildings have not been removed
- Increased incidence of disease

Visit www.heinemann.co.uk/hotlinks for more information

Case study

The Montserrat volcanic eruption, 1997

The volcanic hills in the Caribbean island of Monserrat had been dormant for 400 years before the eruption in 1997. Previously it was regarded as a safe area where farming villages thrived on the fertile volcanic soils.

Build up to the 1997 eruption

1994–95	Small scale earthquakes/Steam and ash eruptions/People evacuated to northern safe zone.
1996–97	The first eruptions/Pyroclastic flows (ash, gas, rock and mud)/50 000 tonnes of ash fell on Southern Montserrat.
June–August 1997	The eruption peaked, with pyroclastic flows of 5 million cubic metres, destroying the capital city (Plymouth) and overunning settlements/23 people were killed and 150 houses destroyed.

The following points are from a letter written by an emergency planning officer visiting Montserrat:

- 'Some roads were 30ft deep in ash'
- 'Whole villages were on fire'
- 'Cars exploded as the heat built up around them'
- 'The only airport was closed'
- 'The eruption caused a storm of grey mud.'

Why do people live in hazardous areas?

- People feel that it 'won't happen to them' and that they are well prepared.
- Some areas, like California (USA), have an excellent climate, superb beaches and a wide range of job opportunities.
- In places like Iceland, geothermal energy can be generated from the volcanic rocks.
- Many minerals and precious stones are found in volcanic areas.
- Volcanic rocks provide mineral-rich fertile soil, which is excellent for agriculture.
- Volcanic activity is often found in spectacular areas of scenery, which provide an excellent opportunity for the development of tourism.

How can the risk of tectonic activity be reduced?

Earthquakes

San Fernando earthquake to cause $30 billion in damages!

In the last 20 years, losses from natural disasters have included 3 million deaths – with earthquakes being the main culprit.

In 1994 the San Fernando valley, Los Angeles, saw yet another example of this. On 17 January a quake of 6.7 magnitude struck the densely-populated valley in northern Los Angeles. Thousands of aftershocks, many in the magnitude 4.0 to 5.0 range, occurred during the next few weeks, further damaging already-affected structures.

Sixty died, but inhabitants may thank the construction laws that it was not more. Los Angeles' construction laws ensured that the buildings are well reinforced so that, even if thrown off their foundations, they are unlikely to fall down. However, in the doomed Maharashtra, western India, more than 10 000 people died in an earthquake of similar magnitude in September of 1993.

The difference? The Indian buildings were of hard volcanic rock – coffins in the making. In Los Angeles, flexible wooden structures – and improved emergency water supplies and communications systems – saved lives.

But that did not save them from damages of an estimated $30 billion (£20 billion) – showing that, no matter how much people prepare, earthquakes still cause problems. You can increasingly build structures that don't kill the inhabitants when a quake strikes but you cannot build structures that won't be damaged.

Key facts

- Earthquakes are unpredictable.
- It is possible to prepare for them.
- Preparation and organization is often better in MEDCs.

Earthquake preparation in Japan

Japan has responded to the threat of earthquakes by:

- making buildings more earthquake resistant
- preparing people by practising rescue drills
- making services such as gas, electricity and water less likely to break
- improving prediction techniques.

Volcanoes

Can volcanic eruptions be predicted?

It is not possible to prevent volcanoes from erupting, and it is difficult to monitor more than a small number of eruptions each year. However, some measures can be taken that help to predict likely eruptions and limit the effects of actual eruptions.

Prediction

Scientists study any changes in the Earth's surface that might give clues to possible volcanic eruptions. Before many eruptions a number of things may occur, including:

- a number of small earth tremors
- bulging, or cracks, appearing on the side of a volcano
- an increase in the ground temperature, with ice and snow melting in mountain areas
- a number of small ash eruptions
- changes in the make up of gases and chemical emissions from the crater.

Many of these events can be detected by sensitive instruments or by satellite technology. Early warning of a likely eruption can then be given.

Limiting the effects of volcanic eruptions

The key to reducing the effects of volcanic eruptions is to make sure that people do not live in the most vulnerable areas. Hazard zoning maps can help by identifying the areas most likely to be affected, and making people aware of the dangers. Many MEDCs now have evacuation procedures in place, and emergency services are trained to deal with the impact of a volcanic eruption. In LEDCs, monitoring and preparation are often less well developed, and consequently the human costs of an eruption are greater.

How important is aid following a tectonic hazard?

Countries don't always have the resources to deal with the effects of earthquakes and volcanoes. Very often many people are injured or left homeless and communications are damaged. Even in MEDCs emergency aid is often given to try and reduce the death toll.

In LEDCs, few buildings are constructed to withstand tectonic hazards, and services are poor. People are often unable to get food and water and outbreaks of disease are common. Consequently the number of deaths and injuries is often greater.

Case Study

LEDC

Aid given to an area following the January 2001 earthquake in western India

On 26 January, an earthquake measuring 7.9 on the Richter Scale occurred in western India. Since then, more than 275 aftershocks have been reported, 19 of which registered above 5.0 on the Richter Scale. Field reports indicated that more than 16 000 have died as a result of the earthquake and over 30 000 have been injured. Local government sources confirm that tens of thousands of people may still be trapped in collapsed buildings.

The government has identified several critical needs … including earth-moving equipment, concrete cutting supplies, and mobile field surgical hospitals … shelter, water and food … .

International governmental assistance

The United States Agency for International Development/Office of US Foreign Disaster Assistance (USAID/OFDA) provided $5 million in emergency humanitarian assistance. An airlift of USAID/OFDA – funded commodities departed Washington, DC on January 28 to meet the immediate needs of 8 000 affected families. The aircraft includes 800 rolls of plastic sheeting, 16 000 blankets, 16 000 5-gallon water containers, 10 water distribution kits, 2 water purification units, 10 generators, 20 light stands, and 20 electrical cords.

The distribution of 100 metric tons of US food commodities began on January 27.

Other international assistance

The European Union (EU) provided $2.78 million in emergency assistance. Additional donations have been made by Britain ($4.5 million), Italy ($2.1 million), Norway ($1.1 million), Netherlands ($420 000), Ireland and Belgium ($920 000), Kuwait ($250 000), South Korea ($100 000) and China ($50 000).

Search and rescue teams from Russia, Switzerland, Britain, Turkey and Germany are operating in the affected area.

▲ *Adapted text from the US Agency for international Development Bureau for humanitarian response (BHR) and office of US Foreign Disaster Assistance (OFDA) India*

Charitable aid

Christian Aid's India Representative, Tom Palakudiyil, says 'the official death toll has reached 30 000 and over 150 000 people are still trapped under collapsed buildings.'

Some of the national organizations that Christian Aid works with in India, such as Churches Auxiliary for Social Action (CASA) and the Voluntary Health Association of India (VHAI), are distributing relief goods and medical help. They are also working with local voluntary groups.

▲ *The Christian Aid Organization*

Making the grade

Using the question effectively

Most questions in geography examinations include information that can be useful in answering the question. Think about the following points and then read the examination question below:

- What information can be obtained from the resource?
- How many marks is each part of the question worth?
- What is each part of the question asking you to do?

a) Opening questions are often just making sure that you have looked at the resource carefully. They are often easy marks BUT check your answers.

b) This question demands some basic knowledge of place. Know your continents. If you are not sure make an educated guess – NEVER leave blank spaces.

c) This question has two commands, *describe* and *explain*. The *describe* part can be done using the map – remember to quote places/continents. The *explain* part is testing your knowledge of plate tectonics *so revision is important*.

Study Figure 1, which shows earthquakes and volcanoes around the Pacific Ocean

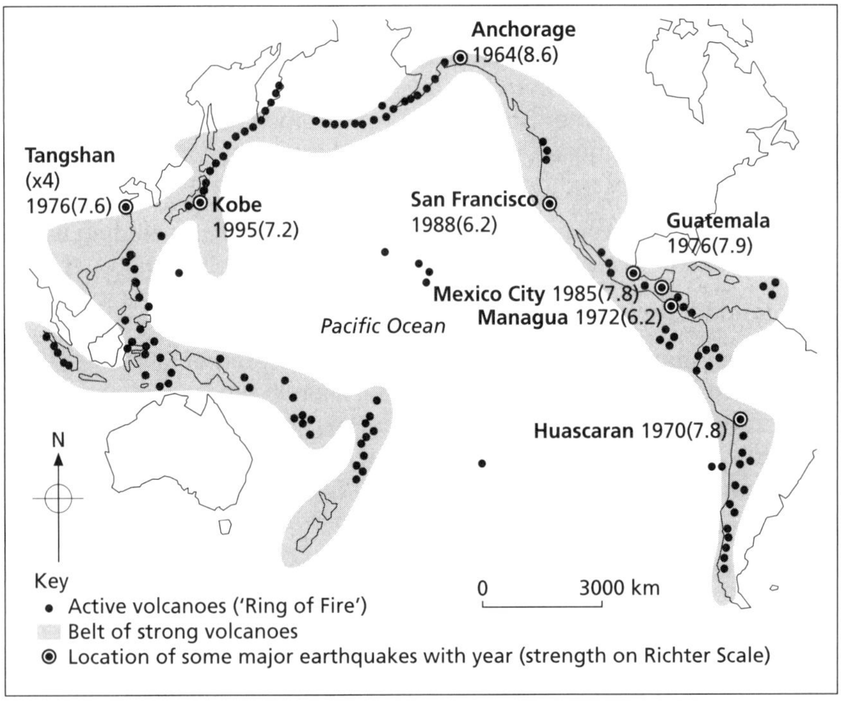

a) i) Which place had the strongest earthquake?
ii) In which year did Kobe have an earthquake measuring 7.2 on the Richter Scale? (2 marks)

b) Name one place affected by an earthquake in North America. (1 mark)

c) Describe and explain the pattern of tectonic activity shown on the map. (6 marks)

d) Using examples you have studied explain why tectonic activity often has different effects. (6 marks)

d) This question is specifically asking for *examples* and the command is *explain* so you need more than simple description. The resource may be helpful – you may have studied some of the places on the map, but *case study revision* will be vital. With little or no locational detail the maximum mark may be 2 or 3.

This question does not specifically ask for LEDC or MEDC examples (some questions will) – the key here is to choose examples that had 'different effects'.

▲ *Figure 1*

Exam practice questions

Study Figure 1, an article describing the Los Angeles Earthquake (1987)

LA Sleeps Rough after Quake

Los Angeles: Thousands of people camped out in parks and on the streets of Los Angeles yesterday, fearing more aftershocks following Thursday's earthquake which killed six people and sparked scores of fires.

Police were put on full alert for the next two days, and were on the lookout for looters. Five people have been accused of stealing from the debris of 20 demolished buildings and hundreds of damaged homes and shops.

About 500 people, forced out of their homes, spent the night in emergency shelters. Three deaths from heart attacks were attributed to the earthquake by safety officials.

A 23-year-old woman student was crushed by a two-tonne slab of falling concrete, a man was trapped 300 feet down a shaft and suffocated under falling earth, and another man was thrown from a second-storey window.

Many of those who spent the warm night sleeping in the open were immigrants with memories of disastrous earthquakes in their homelands. 'We're staying outside until we are really convinced it is safe to go indoors again,' said Mrs Rosa Torres, a Mexican immigrant.

But the city has been rapidly returning to normal despite warnings by seismologists that 'the big one' – an earthquake with a magnitude of at least 8.0 on the Richter scale – is still to come.

Inhabitants accept that there will be more disasters in Los Angeles because the city lies close to the San Andreas fault.

▲ *Figure 1 Adapted from an article in* The Guardian, *3 October 1987*

Use Figure 1 to answer 1(a) and (b).

1 a) Explain why people in Los Angeles were sleeping out of doors after the earthquake. (4 marks)

b) Describe the impacts of the earthquake. (4 marks)

2 a) Explain briefly how earthquakes are caused. (4 marks)

b) Why do earthquakes only occur in certain parts of the world? (4 marks)

c) Draw a labelled diagram to show the main features of a volcanic cone. (3 marks)

3 Why do people live in areas of tectonic activity? (6 marks)

4 Use examples you have studied to explain why the impacts of earthquakes and volcanoes vary. (6 marks)

5 How can the effects of tectonic hazards be reduced? (6 marks)

6 Use examples to explain why aid is important in LEDCs when natural disasters have occurred. (6 marks)

6 Weather hazards

How do storms develop?

Key facts

- All air is under pressure.
- Air pressure is measured in millibars (mb).
- Air moves from high to low pressure.
- Lines joining places of equal pressure are called isobars.
- The closer isobars are together the windier it will be.
- The lower the air pressure the stronger the wind.

What is a depression?

A depression is a low pressure system formed when warm air meets colder air. The boundary where these two air masses meet is called a front. At this point the warm air rises, condenses and clouds form, often bringing rain. The weather associated with a depression is very changeable. Winds will be stronger near the centre of the depression (low pressure centre) and rain clouds will occur as the fronts pass over (see page 62).

What is a tropical storm?

Tropical storms are extreme low pressure systems that build up near the Equator during hot weather and move towards land. Their energy comes form the heat of the atmosphere and the ocean. They are known by different names around the world (e.g. hurricanes, cyclones, typhoons).

How powerful are tropical storms?

The strength of tropical storms is measured using a scale from 1 (minimal damage) to 5 (catastrophic).

The characteristics of a Scale 5 tropical storm are:

- Air pressure – below 920 mb
- Wind speed – over 134 knots
- Storm surge – over 5½ m
- Effect – complete destruction, extensive flooding.

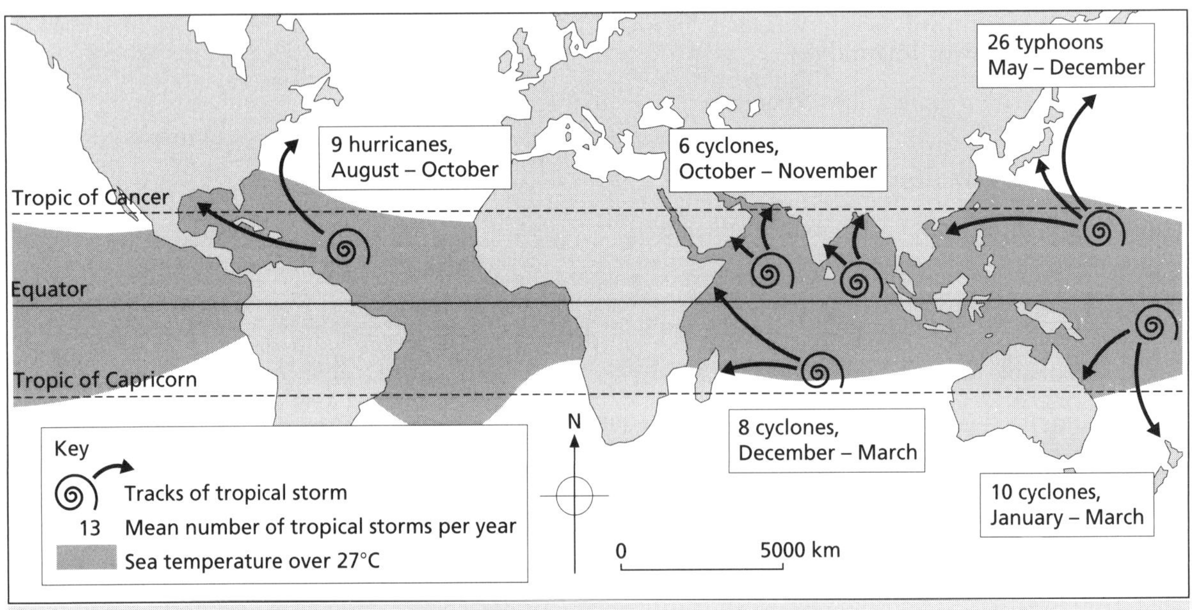

▲ *Location and frequency of tropical storms*

What is the tropical storm hazard?

- **Strong winds** Winds reaching 200 km/h are quite common. These winds can tear up vegetation and push over electricity pylons. Buildings may be damaged, and in poorer areas whole towns can be devastated.
- **Heavy rainfall** Heavy rainfall can rapidly increase river levels and cause flooding. On steeper slopes there is the risk of landslides.
- **Storm surges** The low pressure means that sea-level is very high. The strong winds create huge waves, which push towards coastal areas causing extensive coastal flooding.

Case study

LEDC/MEDC

Hurricane Georges, 1998

In September 1998, Hurricane Georges swept through the northern Caribbean, before moving towards the USA and finally dying out over the southern states of the USA.

The newspaper article describes the effects of the hurricane as it moved across the less economically developed Caribbean islands towards the USA.

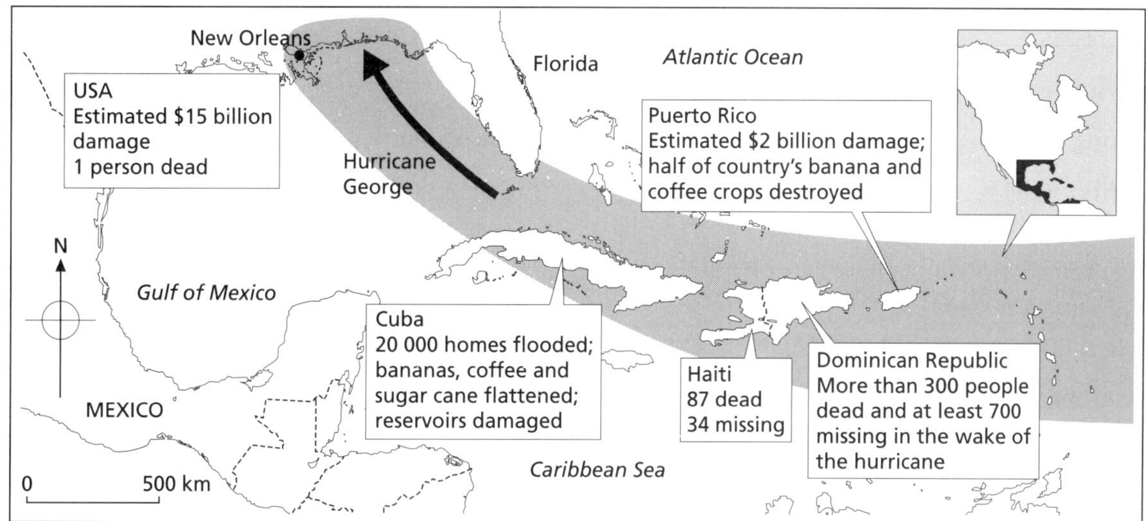

▲ *The path of Hurricane Georges*

Hurricane Georges hits New Orleans

Millions took to the road as Hurricane Georges devastated New Orleans yesterday. 1.5 million people were asked to leave in large-scale evacuations ordered by New Orleans' officials. The 35 000 left temporarily homeless found shelter in dozens of Red Cross shelters.

Hurricane Georges dug deep into the Gulf of Mexico, leaving a trail of sunken houseboats, twisted trees and tangled power lines in Florida. 1.4 million people were ordered to evacuate. But despite massive amounts of damage no casualties were reported in Florida compared to the Dominican Republic death toll of more than 300.

The storm ripped through the Caribbean – the worst hit areas being Haiti and the Dominican Republic. In the city of San Pedro alone 34 000 homes have been damaged and there are food and water shortages. More than 80 per cent of the food crops for these impoverished countries has been wiped out and 100 000 people have been left homeless.

What problems does flooding cause?

Key facts

What are the types of flooding?

River floods These happen regularly and are a result of weather patterns.

Coastal floods These are caused by a combination of weather patterns and sea conditions.

What are the effects of flooding?

Primary effects:
- loss of life
- injury
- loss of land/buildings
- industry/communications destroyed.

Secondary effects:
- loss of shelter
- limited food supply
- contaminated water/disease
- loss of employment/income.

To what extent is flooding a natural hazard?

Flooding can occur as a result of natural factors or be influenced by changes made to the landscape.

Natural factors
- High rainfall
- Higher temperatures causing snow-melt
- Low pressure storms
- High tides and on-shore winds.

Landscape changes that might cause flooding
- Changing slopes
- Removing vegetation
- Changing river patterns/flows
- Building on flat land near rivers.

Global warming could increase the risk of coastal flooding if sea-levels rise.

Bangladesh (LEDC)

Bangladesh is a country that has both river and coastal floods.

River floods result from heavy rainfall and melting snow in the Himalayas. Farmers rely on the floods to supply fine silt to the land, making it fertile and good for the growth of crops.

Coastal floods are created by cyclones which push the water in the Bay of Bengal towards the land, causing a storm surge. This floods the low-lying coastal areas.

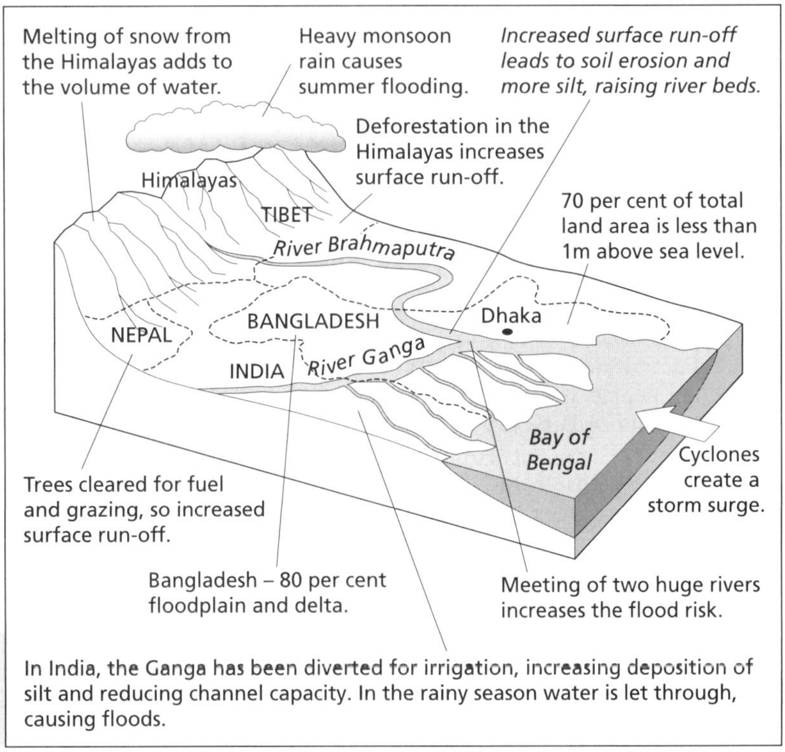

Melting of snow from the Himalayas adds to the volume of water.

Heavy monsoon rain causes summer flooding.

Increased surface run-off leads to soil erosion and more silt, raising river beds.

Deforestation in the Himalayas increases surface run-off.

Himalayas

TIBET

River Brahmaputra

70 per cent of total land area is less than 1m above sea level.

NEPAL

BANGLADESH

Dhaka

INDIA

River Ganga

Bay of Bengal

Cyclones create a storm surge.

Trees cleared for fuel and grazing, so increased surface run-off.

Bangladesh – 80 per cent floodplain and delta.

Meeting of two huge rivers increases the flood risk.

In India, the Ganga has been diverted for irrigation, increasing deposition of silt and reducing channel capacity. In the rainy season water is let through, causing floods.

▶ *The causes of flooding in Bangladesh are due to a mixture of natural and human factors*

Case study

Flooding in Bangladesh

The following adapted newspaper reports illustrate the problem of both river and coastal flooding in Bangladesh.

August 1998
The flooding has lasted nearly three months and more than half of the country is affected. At one stage, the capital city, Dhaka, was under 2 m of water, and power supplies and the sewerage system collapsed. It is estimated that more than a thousand people have died, mainly from dysentery and snake bites.

September 1988
After two weeks of monsoon rains, three-quarters of the country is inundated and nearly 3000 people have died. River levels have risen by over 7 m. Up to 25 million people are homeless with many of them sheltering in makeshift camps. Communications are disrupted, making it difficult for people to reach food supplies, medicine and relief materials. Lack of pure drinking water is reported to have caused outbreaks of diarrhoea, dysentery and cholera.

April 1991
The cyclone has brought devastation to a region where it is difficult to make a living at the best of times. Winds of more than 225 km/h and waves more than 7 m in height swept over the coastal lowlands. People clung to buildings and trees, but the wind was too strong for them to hang on for long. It is estimated that nearly 200 000 people and half a million cattle have drowned. When the floods eventually subside the people will be faced with food shortages and problems of contaminated water. Communications will take months to repair.

Case study

The Mississippi Floods (USA) 1993

Where?

- An area of approximately 8 million hectares was badly affected by the flood.

Why?

- The Mississippi drains water from over 30 per cent of the USA.
- There had been continuous rainfall from April to July saturating soils and leading to rapid overland flow.
- Heavy thunderstorms in June throughout the Midwest delivered record rainfall.
- The Mississippi is fed by over 100 major tributaries. The Missouri and Tennessee rivers carried vast quantities of water into the Mississippi which caused flooding around the **confluences** (where rivers joined).

What happened?

- The river rose to recorded levels causing **levees** to collapse.
- 9000 homes were destroyed and 70 000 people were evacuated.
- 48 people were killed.
- Des Moines and St Louis were left without water and power supplies.
- One million acres of soya bean and corn crops were ruined.
- Roads, railways and bridges were cut off.
- Sewage contaminated water supplies.
- **Sedimentation** blocked navigable channels and disrupted shipping.

There were different opinions about the cause of the floods:
'Rain causes floods, heavy rain causes big floods' (An army engineer suggesting that it was mainly unusually high rainfall that caused the floods.)
'People cause floods by river engineering' (Friends of the Earth, St Louis)
Environmentalists argued that changing the flow of the river and altering the river banks had made the flood worse.

How can areas be protected against flooding?

Case study

LEDC

Can Bangladesh be protected against flooding?

Why does Bangladesh flood?

- Cyclones in the Bay of Bengal cause storm surges
- Monsoon rainfall from June to September
- Melting snow in the Himalayas
- Much of the country is very low-lying

Flood protection

While it is impossible to prevent flooding in Bangladesh, several measures have been introduced as part of the Flood Action Plan, a scheme financed by the World Bank in 1990.

The Flood Action Plan

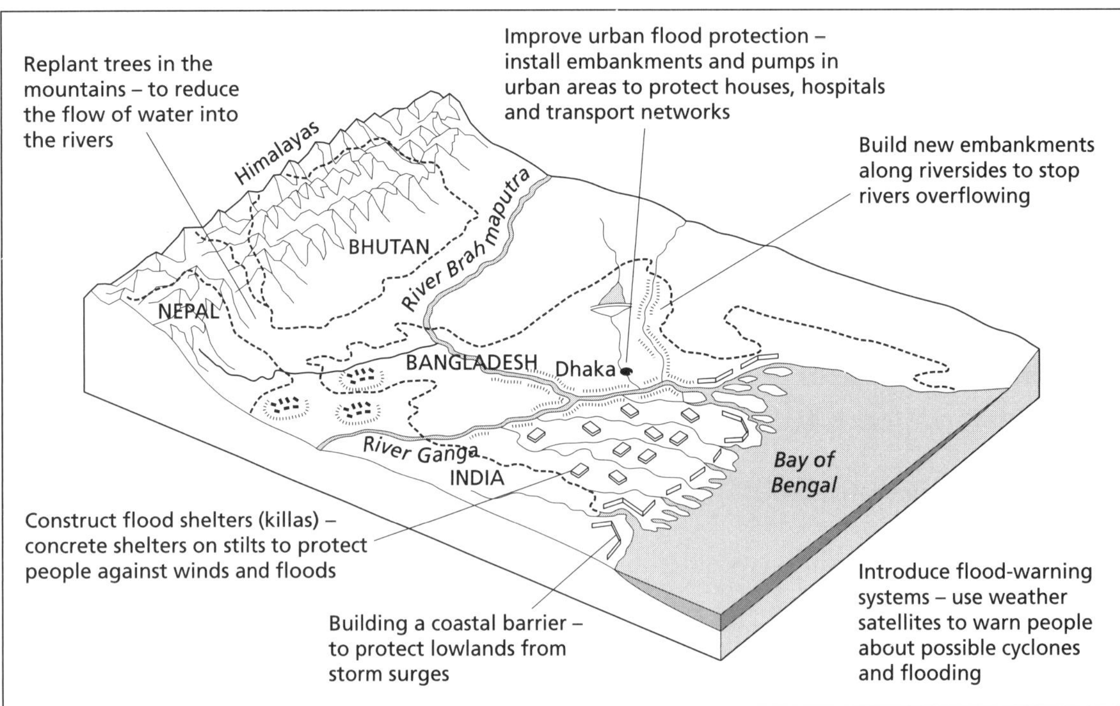

▲ *The flood action plan in Bangladesh*

How well has the scheme worked?

The scheme appears to have had some effect in reducing the impact of flooding, but there are some possible disadvantages.

Advantages

- The flood embankment in Dhaka appears to be reducing the effects of flooding in the city.
- The flood warning system gives some people time to prepare.
- People are more educated about what to do in the event of a flood.
- A number of shelters have been built.
- The building of embankments has created jobs.

Disadvantages

- At £100 million a year, maintenance costs are very high for a poor country.
- Pumping systems do not always separate floodwater from sewage, creating problems of disease.
- Embankments create pools of stagnant water which attract mosquitoes and can lead to disease.
- Stopping water from going into one area can create flood problems elsewhere.
- The pattern of flooding has changed, and this affects the farming and fishing communities.

Case study

MEDC

Why was the Thames Flood Barrier built?

In 1953 a combination of high tides and a storm surge from the North Sea caused severe flooding in Eastern England. Over 300 people were killed and the cost of damage estimated at £50 million. Many people affected lived in the Thames estuary and afterwards it was realised that had London been flooded it would have been catastrophic.

The following press release by the Greater London Council makes this point:
'The severe flooding of London could be the greatest natural disaster this country is likely to experience. More than a million people could be at risk and thousands of homes would be destroyed. Transport would come to a standstill and many parts of London would be under water for days. The cost of such an event would run into thousands of million of pounds.'

Because of this risk a Flood Defence Scheme for London was put in place, the main part of this being the Thames Barrier.

THAMES BARRIER PROTECTING LONDON

The Thames Barrier is part of a flood defence scheme for London which includes downstream bank-raising in the Thames estuary, flood gates on smaller rivers and upstream bank-raising in the tidal Thames. The Thames Barrier flood gates are raised to form a solid barrier should an unusually high tide be predicted. The Barrier spans 520 metres across the river. It consists of ten separate movable steel gates, each pivoting and supported between concrete piers.

▲ *Extract from Thames Barrier leaflet, 2002*

Case study

LEDC

Why is emergency relief needed after a natural disaster?

Hurricane Mitch, 1998

Hurricane Mitch hit in October 1998 and devastated huge areas of Nicaragua, Honduras, Guatemala and El Salvador.
Over 10 000 people were feared dead and millions were left homeless. The hurricane brought high winds and torrential rain for several days, causing extensive flooding and landslides. Bridges, roads and buildings were all destroyed, and in some areas entire villages were demolished. In Honduras alone, almost 70 per cent of the year's crops were ruined and over 560 000 people were living in makeshift shelters.

Emergency needs

Threat of disease – Damage to the water supply system meant there was a shortage of safe drinking water. Outbreaks of diseases including cholera and diarrhoea were feared. Contaminated water also increased the spread of diseases such as malaria. Water purification tablets and portable water pumps were needed whilst long term repairs were made.
Food and medical shortages – Food supplies were low and crops were destroyed. Most medicine reserves were used in the immediate emergency and replacements were urgently needed
Infrastructure repairs – Destruction of roads and bridges was restricting the distribution of food, medicines and other supplies. Repair work on roads and bridges was essential.
Homelessness – Materials were needed to build temporary shelters for the millions of homeless people.

▲ *Extract from article in* Global Eye, *1998, No. 8 published by Worldaware*

Making the grade

Reading the weather map

The weather can be shown using a weather map, called a synoptic chart, or using a satellite image which shows cloud patterns.

Examiners often use weather maps to test whether candidates can:

- read maps by using the key
- understand what weather maps say about changing weather patterns.

Weather maps use three different techniques to show the weather:

1 Isobars (black lines) which join up places of equal air pressure
2 Weather station symbols which show general conditions at particular places
3 Fronts (warm or cold) which show the leading edge of a block of air.

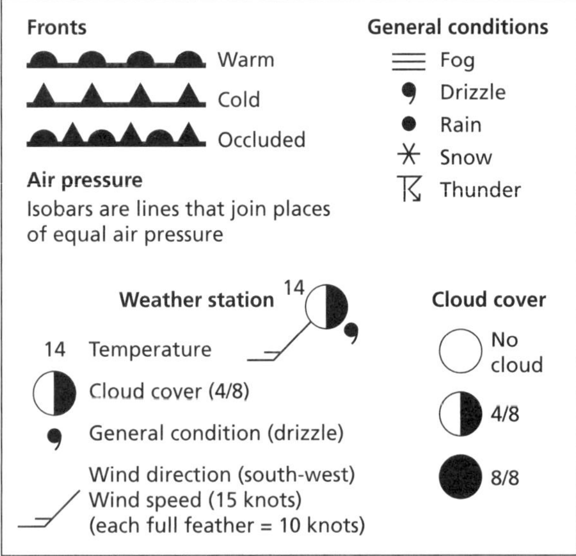

▲ *Figure 1 Symbols found on a weather map*

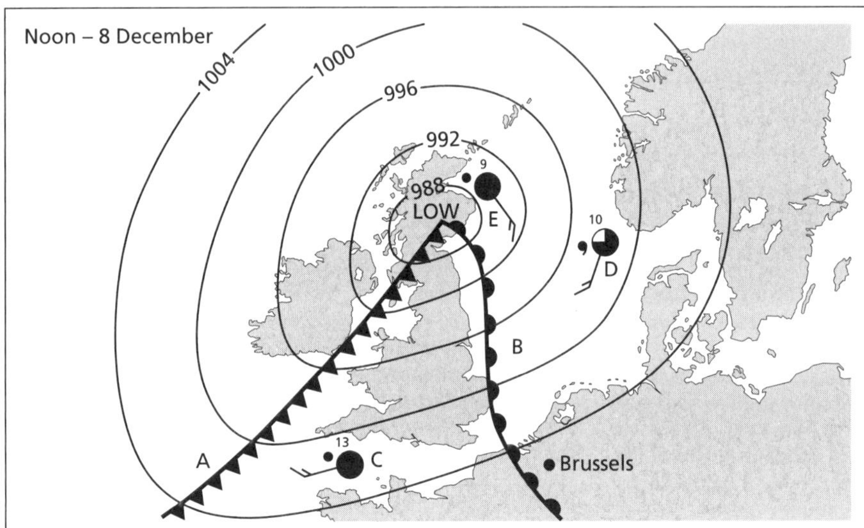

◀ *Figure 2 Synoptic chart for a depression*

Key facts

- Weather stations give a good indication about local weather conditions.
- The lower the air pressure the stronger the wind.
- Isobars closer together indicate stronger winds.
- Fronts are where warm air rises and this often brings cloud and rain.
- Cold fronts usually bring more violent rainstorms.

Questions

Using the weather map (Figure 2):

a) Name the features at A and B.

b) Describe the weather conditions at weather stations C, D and E.

c) How is the weather in Brussels likely to change in the next 24 hours?

Exam practice questions

News update

Mozambique, 2000

Problems began in early February when rainfall was much heavier than usual. This became worse as two intense tropical cyclones hit the country. Cyclone Eline arrived in the last week of February, bringing high winds and torrential rain. In March, Gloria brought yet more rain and flooding. Estimates put the total rainfall in February at over 1000 mm (7 times higher than normal).

Flooding devastated much of central and southern Mozambique. As the rivers overflowed, land was not just submerged under water, but also under layers of mud and silt. TV news reports showed thousands of people on roof tops and in trees surrounded by flood water, waiting to be rescued by boat or helicopter. Two months later the floodwater is at last beginning to recede, but the damage it has left behind will take years (and billions of dollars) to repair. In the short term, there is a continuing threat of water-borne disease like cholera and malaria and an urgent need to re-home and feed up to a million people.

Help is still desperately needed. Homes, roads, bridges, railways, schools and clinics need to be rebuilt. Water supplies and irrigation schemes need to be restored and made safe. Over a quarter of the farmland has been affected – over 80 per cent of Mozambique's people rely on farming. Much foreign aid has arrived, notably food, blankets, seeds, farming tools and medicines.

Extract from* www.globaleye.org.uk *published by Worldaware.

Datafile

Deaths:	700+
Missing:	50 000+
Help needed for:	1–2 million people
Food aid needed for:	0.5–1 million people
Homeless people:	250 000 – 500 000
Crops/tools lost:	124 000 households
Schools destroyed:	600 (120 000 children displaced)

▲ *Figure 1 Location map of Mozambique*

1 Study the extract from *Global Eye* above to answer question 1.

a) i) How much rain fell in February?

ii) How many schools were destroyed?

iii) What do most of Mozambique's population rely on to earn a living? (3 marks)

b) Why was emergency aid needed after the flood? (4 marks)

c) Why does it often take a long time for LEDCs like Mozambique to recover from floods? (6 marks)

2 Describe the hazards associated with tropical storms. (4 marks)

3 'Flooding is often caused by a combination of physical and human factors.' Use examples to explain this statement. (6 marks)

4 Describe the advantages and disadvantages of one flood management scheme you have studied. (6 marks)

7 Water and food supply

Why do some areas not have enough food and water?

Which parts of the world are short of food?

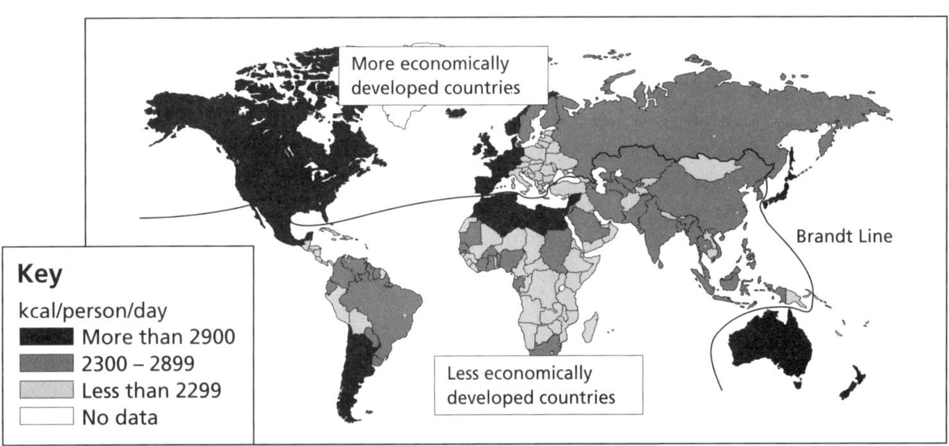

▲ *Global distribution of food supplies*

Where are the hungry people?

Food shortages are most common in parts of Asia (Bangladesh/Pakistan) and Africa. One third of all children south of the Sahara in Africa are malnourished.

What are the problems of poor water supply?

Rachel Anton lives in Tanzania. She spends five hours a day collecting water from puddles and streams. Her family frequently get stomach problems because the water is contaminated.

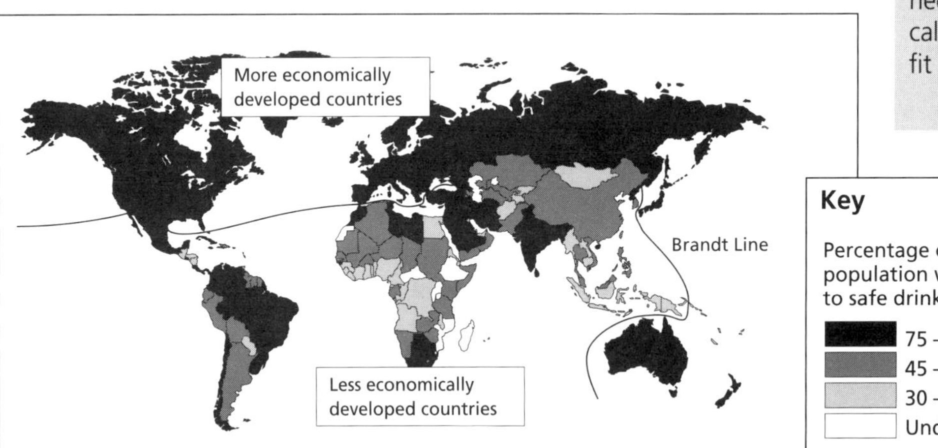

▲ *Global distribution of access to safe water*

Key facts

- More than 1 billion people in the world suffer from serious hunger.
- It is estimated that around 24 000 people die each day from the effects of hunger.
- Nearly 50 per cent of the world's people lack access to safe water.
- Contaminated water causes 80 per cent of disease in developing countries and kills 10 million people a year.

Remember

The average person needs about 2500 calories a day to keep fit and healthy.

What are the causes of poor food supply?

- Poverty means that in times of drought people cannot buy food to stay alive.
- Lack of available land affects millions of people in rural areas.
- Commercial farming has reduced food production in many areas.
- War frequently disrupts farming. People are prevented from working the land and from planting food.
- Poor transportation is a cause of poor food supplies in some places.
- Lack of resources in rural areas may result in low crop yields.
- Overgrazing, and the consequent loss of vegetation cover, leaves the ground bare and soil is eroded.
- Drought, caused by too little rain, unreliable rainfall and the mismanagement of land and water supplies, probably causes most hunger each year.

What are the causes of poor water supply?

- Lack of rainfall can affect the supply and storage of water.
- Poverty means that in many LEDCs people cannot afford to buy clean water.
- Many parts of the world do not have the infrastructure to distribute and purify drinking water.
- In some areas water is rationed and agriculture and industry are supplied first.
- The rapid growth of urban areas in LEDCs is making it increasingly difficult to supply people with water.
- In many parts of the world people are forced to drink contaminated water or use polluted rivers.

What is desertification?

The term 'desertification' was first used in 1949 to describe the way that semi-arid areas were turning into deserts in some parts of the world.

Definitions

Drought A lack of rainfall over a long period of time

Desertification The spread of desert-like conditions

Case study

LEDC

Desertification in Africa

The Sahel

The Sahel is a semi-arid region to the south of the Sahara desert. Total rainfall is low in this region and there is a dry period each year. People survive in this area by herding animals and growing subsistence crops. Trees are cut down for fuel.

Causes of desertification

Natural processes

- Climate change leading to less rainfall
- Loss of vegetation leading to soil erosion

Human activity

- Overgrazing and cultivation leading to soil exhaustion and erosion
- Deforestation leading to the ground being left exposed to wind erosion

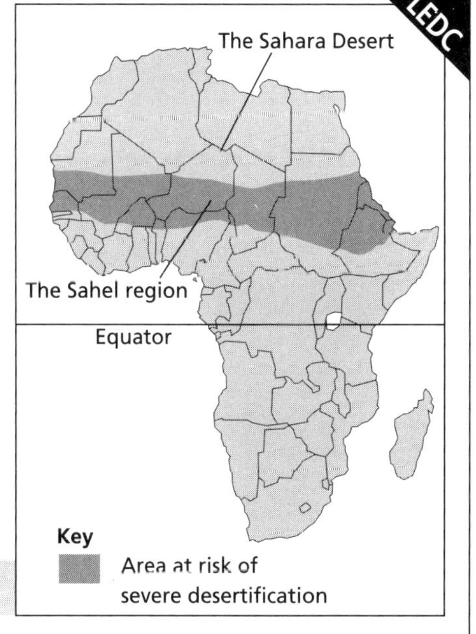

▶ *The Sahel*

What are the effects of poor food and water supplies?

Impacts of poor food supply

More than 1 billion people in the world suffer from serious hunger. Poverty and hunger go together. Forty per cent of those who are hungry are subsistence farmers from the poorest countries in the world. In 2000 the Food and Agricultural Organization (FAO) estimated that 20 million people in East Africa were suffering from serious food shortages, including:

- 300 000 from Eritrea suffering from drought
- 3 million from Sudan because of civil war
- 800 000 from Tanzania because of unreliable rainfall.

The effects of malnutrition:

- **Kwashiorkor** leads to swollen limbs, a bloated stomach, tiredness and lack of growth.
- **Marasmus** leads to diarrhoea and low immunity to other diseases.
- **Anaemia** leads to extreme tiredness where people cannot work.
- **Blindness** can be a result of a lack of Vitamin A and affects 250 000 children a year.

Definitions

Undernutrition
Too little food

Malnutrition
Lack of the right kinds of food

Case study

LEDC

Food shortages in Africa, 2002

What's going on?

The region is currently facing an estimated deficit of three million tonnes of maize for the food year April 2002–March 2003. Despite the drought in 2001 and 2002, there have also been major floods. These have destroyed crops and brought additional disease to humans and livestock.

The following articles are adapted from 'World Vision' (September 2002) and illustrate the problems of food shortages in Africa:

'Across seven countries in southern Africa an estimated 13 million people are currently facing starvation. In Malawi, where life expectancy is just 37 years, drought and poverty have meant that many farmers have grown little food for two years. If they cannot grow food they have little to eat and nothing to sell. Lack of nutrition makes people vulnerable to sickness so they cannot work. It is a vicious circle.'

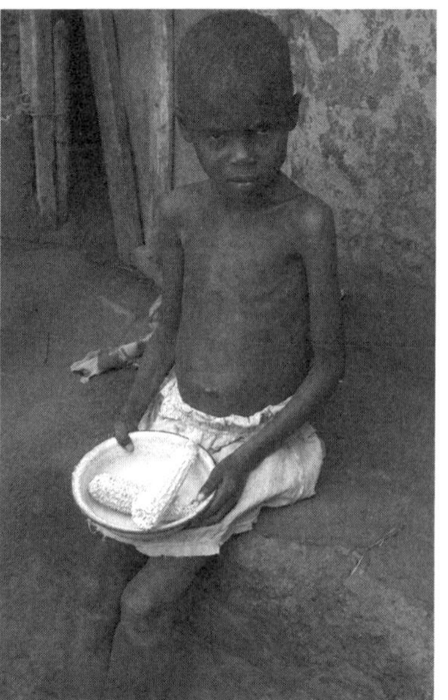

▲ *Munneranji*

'Munneranji, aged seven, holds a bowl of corn cobs she has collected from village waste dumps in Malawi. Her mother, who has three other children, grinds the cobs down to make a sawdust-like flour with a bitter, vinegary odour. The family even grind banana roots into a porridge; it has no nutritional value but makes them feel full. Munneranji doesn't go to school; it closed because there was too much hunger in the community. She's got scabies (a skin parasite), and her chest is so thin her beating heart can be seen beneath it.'

Impacts of poor water supply

Water supply can be a problem in two ways:

1 Some areas have insufficient water or suffer from droughts.

2 In many LEDCs people are forced to drink contaminated water.

Key fact

Article 24 of the 1989 United Nations Convention on the Rights of the Child states that every child should have the right to clean drinking water.

The problem of drought

In many parts of the world, getting enough water for drinking, cooking and washing is a constant problem, and finding water for crops and animals an added pressure. Even when water is available it may be miles away and take hours to collect. The following article shows the effects of water shortages and how they link to food shortages.

Drought in Africa

Lack of rainfall has brought drought to large parts of central and northern Africa. In Chad more than 3000 have died in the past three months in what is believed to be the worst drought this century. In Mali nearly 2 million people are at risk and infant mortality rates are increasing as disease takes a hold. Cattle losses in Mauritania have reached over 60 per cent. In eastern Africa both Ethiopia and Sudan are suffering from poor harvests and more than 6 million people in Ethiopia are at risk of famine. Levels of disease are increasing rapidly in overcrowded relief camps where many children have already died.

▶ *Adapted news article, consequences of drought in the Sahel region, 1986*

The problem of contaminated water

The World Commission on Water stated in March 1999 that:

- 1.4 billion people live without clean drinking water.
- 2.3 billion people lack adequate sanitation.
- 7 million people die yearly from diseases linked to water quality.
- Levels of access to safe water are often higher in urban areas in LEDCs because it is easier to organize supplies.
- However, the continued growth of urban areas puts increasing pressure on water supplies and forces people to drink contaminated water.

The following article shows the link between clean water, sanitation and levels of health.

Poor Water, Poor Health

There is a clear link between the incidence of disease and the availability of clean drinking water and adequate sanitation facilities.

Almost ten million children a year die from infectious and parasitic diseases, many of which could be eradicated if clean water and proper sewage disposal systems were available. These two basic facilities go together, for supplies of extra water can actually spread more disease unless adequate sanitation is provided too.

In those areas which have been supplied with these basic facilities, health has usually improved dramatically, especially where the physical installation is accompanied by health education.

While it is unrealistic to think of supplying everyone in the world with a bath/shower unit and flush toilet, the provision of clean water and sanitation makes good economic sense, for it would reduce the costly burden of disease and increase the ability of millions of people to lead more productive lives.

▲ *From 'Water and Health – Cholera's grim warning',* Understanding Global Issues, *published by ESP Ltd*

How can food and water supplies be improved?

Food and water projects can vary in scale and include:

- Multi-million dollar water management projects, which require massive engineering works.
- Small-scale projects, which are village based and often funded by charitable donations.

Key facts

- The aim of the 1996 World Food Summit was to reduce the number of undernourished people by 50 per cent in 20 years.
- The aim of the United Nations 'Water Decade 80s' was to make sure that every person has access to safe water.

Case study

LEDC

The Aswan Dam, Egypt

In the 1960s the Aswan Dam was built to control the River Nile and provide electricity and improved food and water supply to Egypt.

Advantages of the Aswan Dam

- Flooding is controlled and managed.
- Irrigated land has increased.
- Crop yields have increased, with double cropping.
- Cash crops – sugar cane, cotton, vegetables – have increased, bringing in more money.
- There is all-year river navigation.
- Fishing, recreation and tourism are also possible on Lake Nasser.
- Hydro-electric power has helped industry to develop.
- More towns and villages have electricity and clean water.

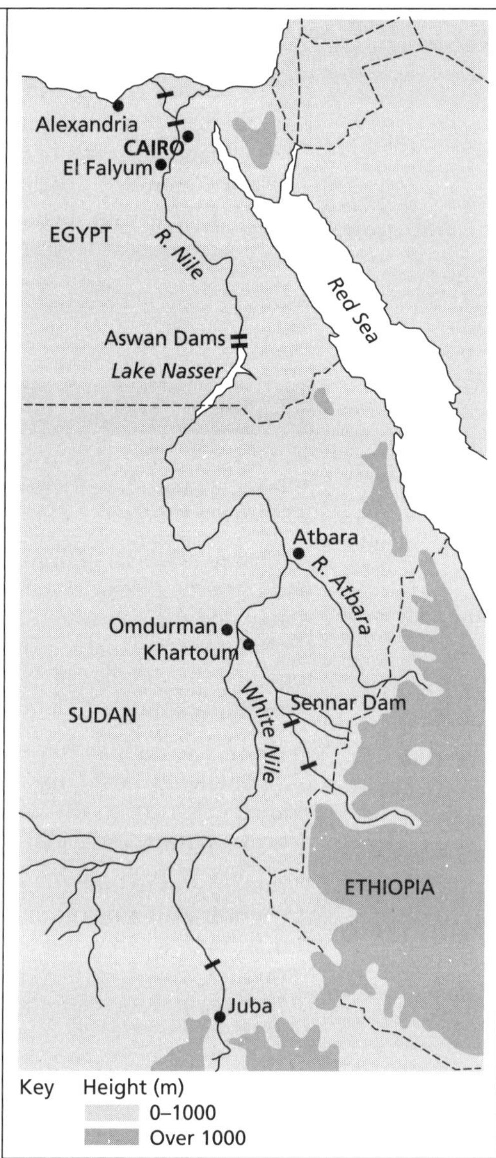

Problems resulting from the Aswan Dam

- Fertile silt is no longer spread over the land.
- Chemical fertilizers are needed.
- Water is shallow and slow-moving – bilharzia (from river snails) and other diseases have increased.
- Agricultural fertilizers and pesticides as well as herbicides, domestic and industrial waste pollute the river water.
- Salt from irrigation water collects and crop yields fall.
- Lagoons behind the sand bars used for fishing (a good source of protein), are disappearing.
- In Lake Nasser, fish and silt are trapped behind the dam.

▲ *The advantages and disadvantages of the Aswan Dam*

Case study

MEDC

The Central Valley Project, California (USA)

California has a seasonal pattern of rainfall and a distinct dry period in the summer. More rain falls in the north but much of the most suitable agricultural land is in the south. Consequently, in order to make good use of the land, irrigation is needed.

The project

The Central Valley project was built by the Government to allow water to be stored and then transported along aqueducts. A network of canals takes water to the drier areas and makes agriculture possible. The Central Valley is now used to grow a wide variety of crops, including fruit, vegetables and cotton. Beef cattle are also reared on the irrigated grasslands.

The problems

- The project cost millions of dollars to build.
- The cost of the water is high.
- The reservoirs silt up and need constant maintenance.
- Levels of salt in the water are increasing in some areas, polluting the land and killing animal life.

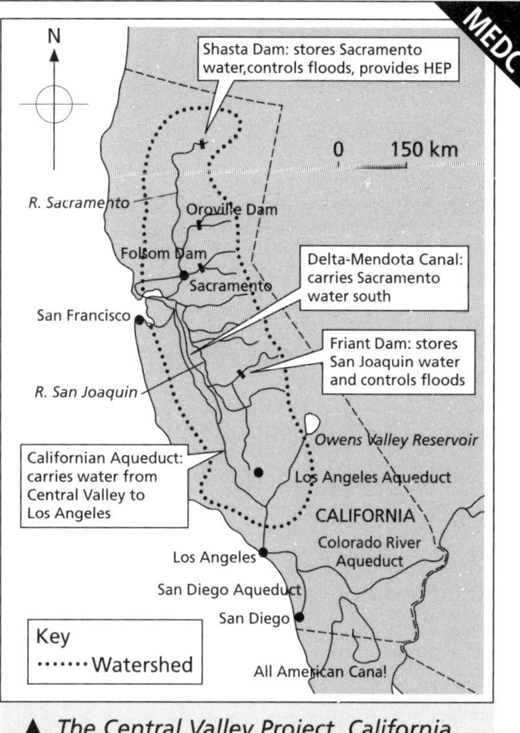

▲ *The Central Valley Project, California*

Case study

LEDC

FARM-Africa – Improving food and water supplies

FARM-Africa is a charitable organization that has been working with poor rural African farmers since 1985.

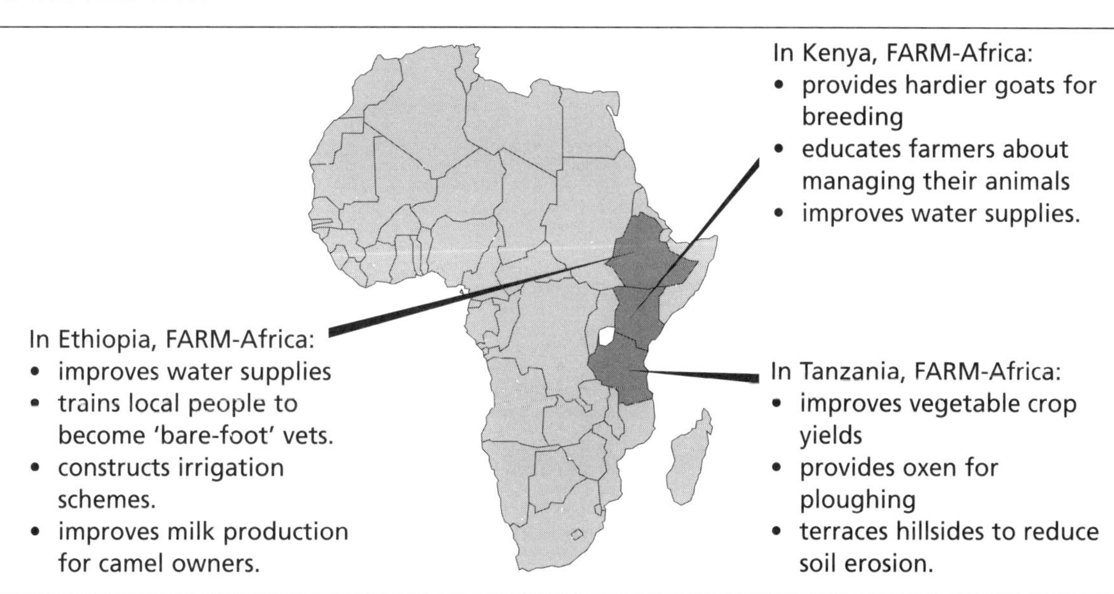

▲ *FARM-Africa*

Projects like FARM-Africa are sustainable and help small communities to increase their food output. However, critics suggest that larger scale projects have the potential to affect a greater number of people.

Visit www.heinemann.co.uk/hotlinks for more information

Making the grade

Using photographs

Examiners often use photographs as a resource in examination questions.

Photographs can be used:

- For skills-based questions which ask for a description or identification of key points.
- As a stimulus resource to show understanding or knowledge of a particular topic.

Careful and detailed use of a photograph can provide a wide range of descriptive and analytical ideas.

Look at the following example:

a) Use the photograph (Figure 1) to suggest why contaminated water is a major problem in LEDCs. (6 marks)

b) Use examples you have studied to describe a way that water supply in LEDCs could be improved. (6 marks)

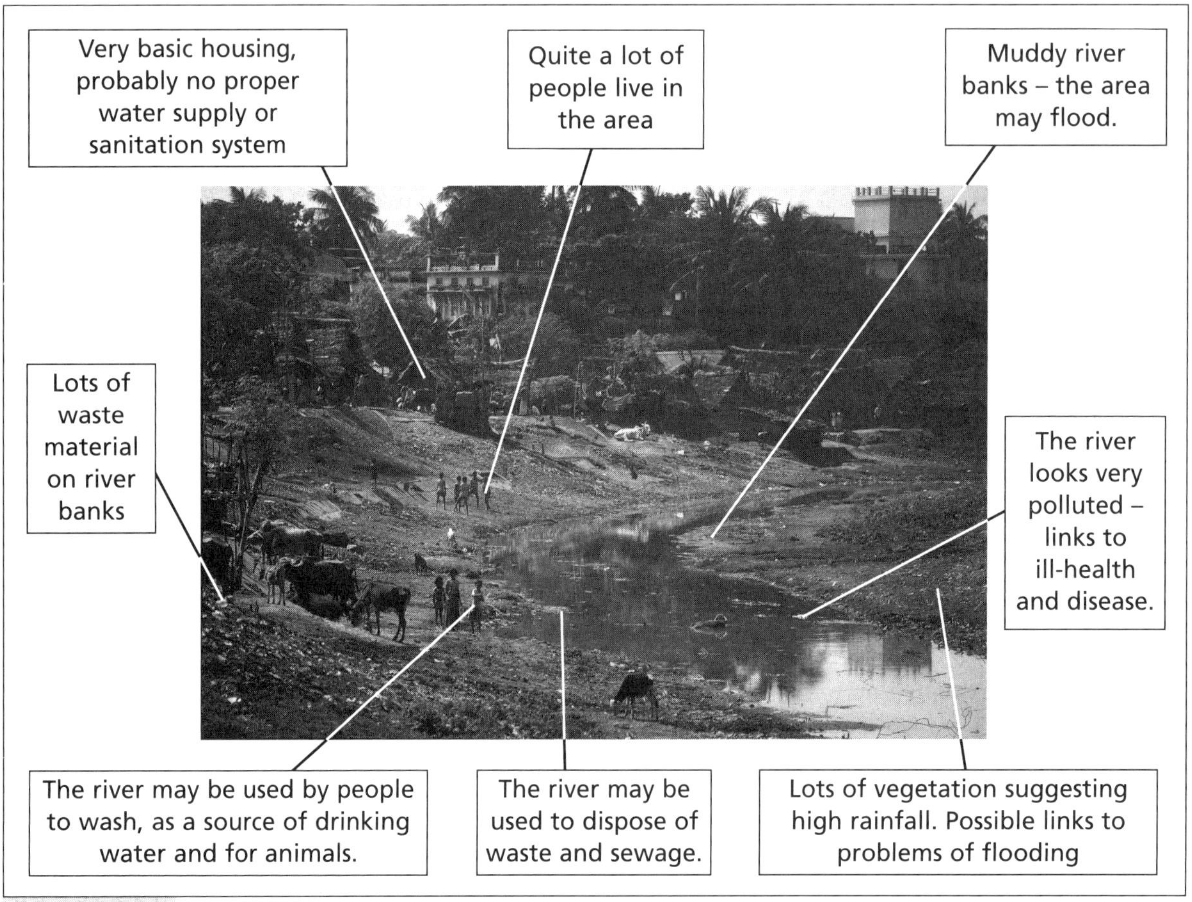

Very basic housing, probably no proper water supply or sanitation system

Quite a lot of people live in the area

Muddy river banks – the area may flood.

Lots of waste material on river banks

The river looks very polluted – links to ill-health and disease.

The river may be used by people to wash, as a source of drinking water and for animals.

The river may be used to dispose of waste and sewage.

Lots of vegetation suggesting high rainfall. Possible links to problems of flooding

▲ *Figure 1*

Remember

Practise using photographs by putting them in the centre of a page and identifying the main points around the edge.

Exam practice questions

Use Figure 1 to answer questions 1(a) and (b).

1 a) Explain how a lack of food can lead to a downward spiral towards starvation. (4 marks)

b) Describe two causes of hunger. (4 marks)

c) Using examples you have studied explain how food supplies could be improved in LEDCs. (6 marks)

2 a) What is meant by desertification? (2 marks)

b) Explain how desertification is often the result of both physical and human factors. (6 marks)

Too little food
Malnourishment
Little energy
Less food grown
Malnutrition

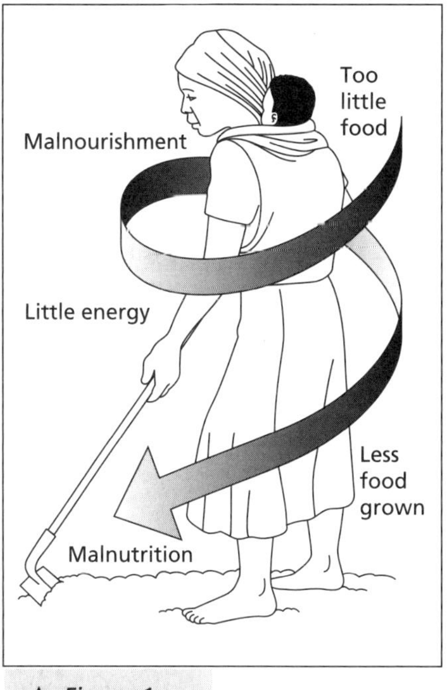

▲ *Figure 1*

3 Study Figure 2, an aid advertisement from Oxfam to answer questions 3(a) and (b).

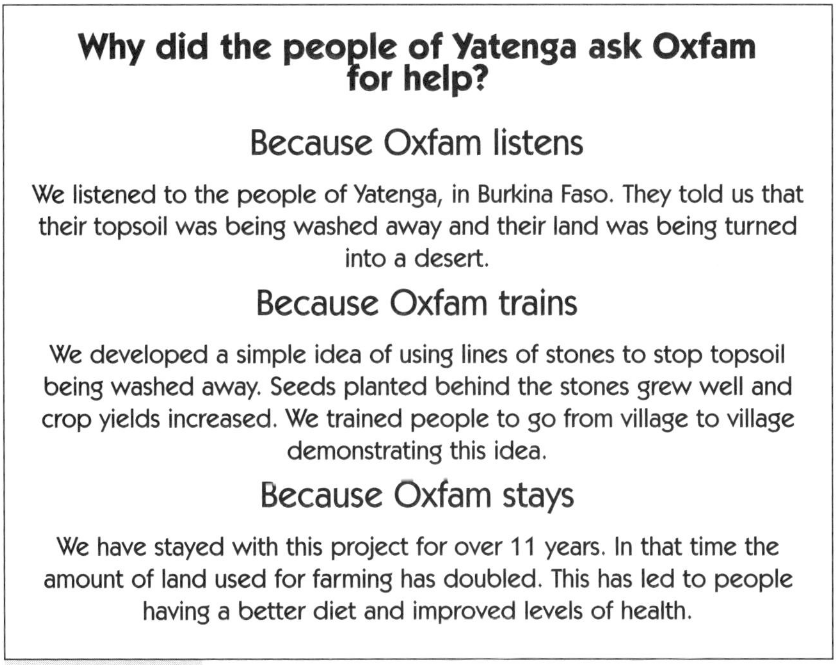

Why did the people of Yatenga ask Oxfam for help?
Because Oxfam listens
We listened to the people of Yatenga, in Burkina Faso. They told us that their topsoil was being washed away and their land was being turned into a desert.
Because Oxfam trains
We developed a simple idea of using lines of stones to stop topsoil being washed away. Seeds planted behind the stones grew well and crop yields increased. We trained people to go from village to village demonstrating this idea.
Because Oxfam stays
We have stayed with this project for over 11 years. In that time the amount of land used for farming has doubled. This has led to people having a better diet and improved levels of health.

▲ *Figure 2*

a) What was the problem in Burkina Faso? (2 marks)

b) Explain how the project might improve living standards in the area. (6 marks)

4 a) What are the possible problems of contaminated water? (4 marks)

b) Using one or more examples explain how water supplies could be improved. (6 marks)

8 Pressures on the physical environment

How do physical processes shape natural landscapes?

Examiners can ask about the processes involved in any natural landscape.

This could include:
- Coastal landscapes
- River landscapes
- Limestone landscapes
- Glaciated landscapes.

You are not expected to know about all of these different landscapes – the important thing is to understand the processes involved and then be able to apply them to your chosen example.

It is also helpful to be able to appreciate why your chosen landscapes may attract visitors.

Definitions

Weathering The breaking of rocks by the action of weather, chemicals or plants

Erosion The wearing down or removal of material by water, ice or wind

Deposition The laying down of material by water, ice or wind

Limestone landscapes

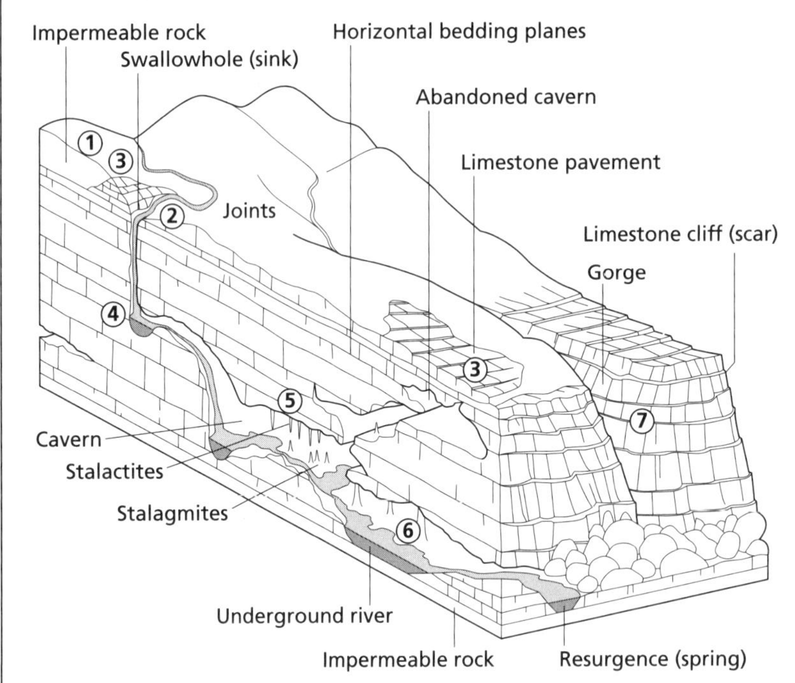

The formation of limestone scenery

1. Rainfall is high. The upper slopes are impermeable (do not allow water to pass through).
2. Surface streams quickly form and flow downhill. When they reach the permeable limestone they disappear down enlarged joints (potholes or swallow holes).
3. Rain falling on the limestone dissolves the rock as it trickles through the cracks and joints leaving the limestone looking like a 'pavement'.
4. Joints are slowly enlarged by solution and erosion to form caves. After heavy rain, fast-flowing streams erode rock channels.
5. Calcium is released by the chemical reaction between rainwater, limestone and carbon dioxide. The calcium is either deposited on cave walls or grows slowly as stalactities (from the roof) and stalagmites (from the floor).
6. A saturated layer or water table forms in limestone above the impermeable rocks. Sudden rises in rainfall can fill the cave systems. In the valley, the river bubbles out again at a resurgence (spring).
7. Valleys in limestone are often steep-sided gorges. Bare limestone cliffs (scars) outcrop on the valley sides.

Weathering is a major process in the formation of limestone landscapes.
Physical weathering The action of heat and water
Chemical weathering Breakdown of rocks by chemical action
Biological weathering The action of plant roots and animals

▲ *Limestone scenery*

Remember

Think about why limestone landscapes might attract visitors.

Coastal landscapes

Erosion is a major process in coastal areas. The main types of erosion are:

- **Hydraulic action** The action of waves crashing against the cliffs
- **Attrition** Rock fragments rubbing against each other
- **Corrasion** Waves hurling material against cliffs
- **Corrosion** Cliffs being dissolved by seawater

Headland erosion

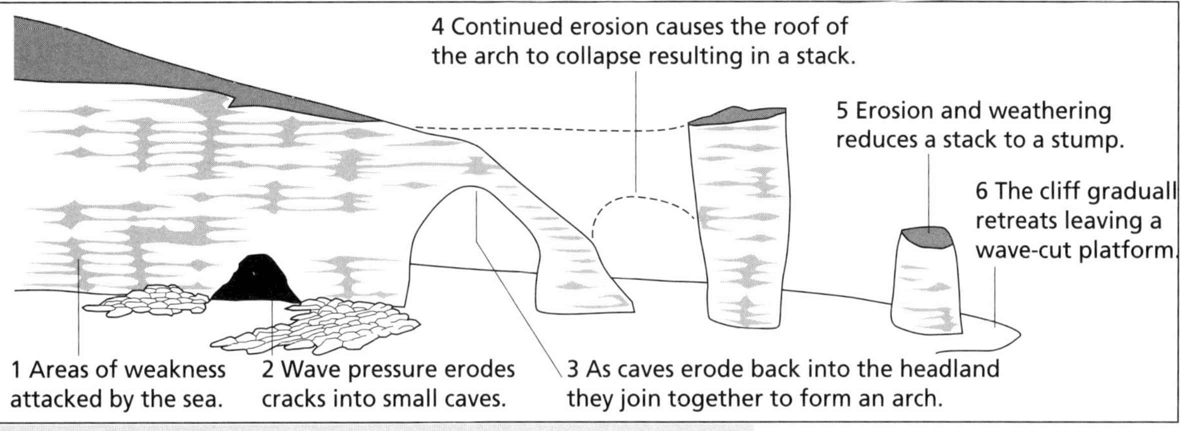

▲ *The erosion of a chalk headland (e.g. Old Harry Rocks, Dorset)*

Longshore drift: the movement of material

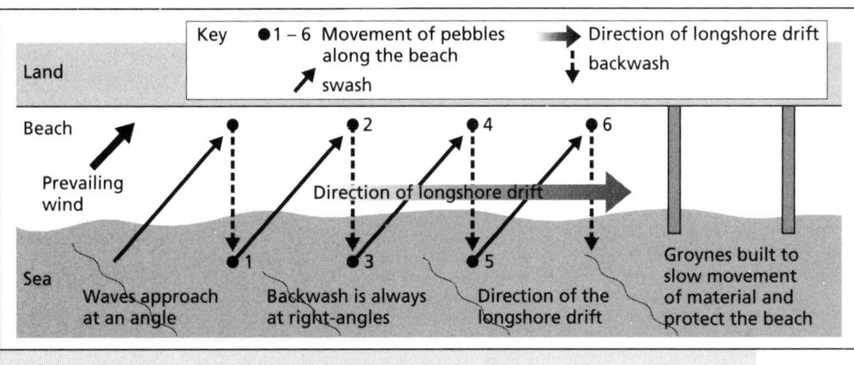

▲ *The process of longshore drift*

Remember

It is often useful to use an annotated sketch when describing physical processes and features.

Coastal deposition – the formation of a spit

Where there is a curve on the coastline, material is often deposited forming a spit.

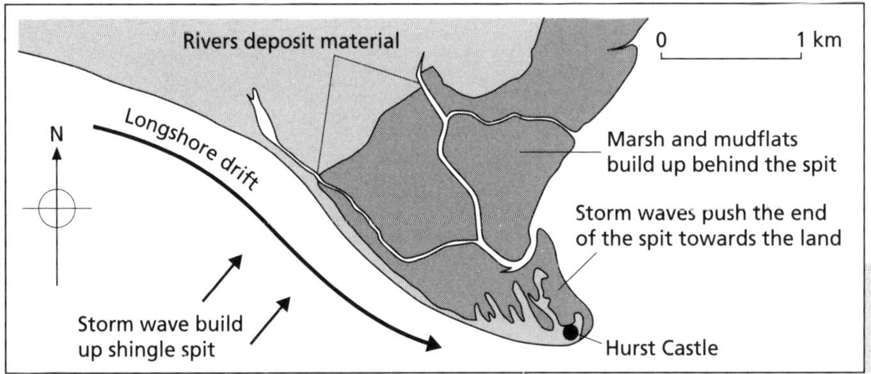

◀ *The formation of a spit (e.g. Hurst Castle Spit, Hampshire)*

Remember

Think about why coastal landscapes attract visitors.

What are the effects of the growth of recreation and tourism?

Why has there been a growth in recreation and tourism?

- An increase in the length of paid holidays
- Greater wealth – more money to spend on holidays
- An increase in car ownership
- Improved communications
- Increased awareness of different places
- An increasing proportion of retired people.

> *Definitions*
>
> **National parks** Areas of outstanding scenery where human activity is controlled
>
> **Honeypot site** Places with special appeal that attract large numbers of visitors

What are national parks?

National parks in England and Wales were set up in 1951 to:

- protect areas of great natural beauty
- promote the enjoyment of recreational activity.

National parks in England and Wales have permanent populations and most of the land is privately owned, which can lead to planning and tourism conflicts.

National parks in England and Wales

Example of a honeypot site: Lake Windermere (Lake District)

Why does the area attract visitors?

- Attractive scenery
- Leisure facilities
- Historical interest
- Sporting activities

Pressures on the area

- Traffic congestion
- Overcrowded towns
- Litter/noise
- Building development

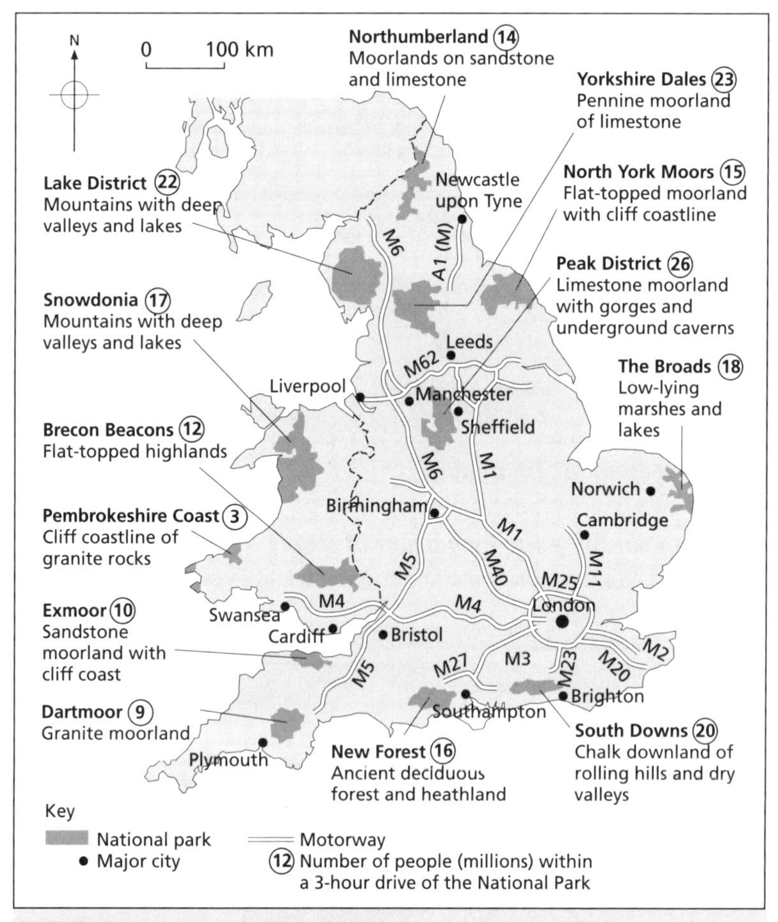

▲ *Location and characteristics of National Parks in England and Wales*

Case study

MEDC

The Lake District National Park

The Lake District National Park was formed in 1951 and has become one of the most popular national parks in the world.
In 1999 the area was visited by over 20 million people. As well as being an important visitor destination the area also has a resident population of over 40 000 people.

Why do people visit the Lake District?

- Spectacular scenery including mountains, rivers and coastal areas.
- The area has good access with motorway links.
- There are many small, attractive settlements.
- There is good opportunity for activity holidays including:
  - walking
  - climbing
  - water sports
  - horse riding.

The effects of recreational development

The most popular footpaths and lakesides are being eroded.

Local shops have been replaced by gift shops.

Overuse of the lakes causes pollution and conflict between different users.

Demand for holiday homes pushes up local house prices.

Money from tourism helps the upkeep of the area.

Recreation and tourism creates many direct and indirect jobs.

Tourism gives people the opportunity to experience and understand the environment.

Tourism gives a boost to many local industries.

Case study

Yosemite National Park, Western USA

With nearly four million visitors each year Yosemite National Park comes under considerable pressure.

> 'YOSEMITE NATIONAL PARK embraces almost 1200 square miles of scenic wild lands set aside in 1890 to preserve a portion of the central Sierra Nevada that stretches along California's eastern flank. The park ranges from 2000 feet to more than 13 000 feet above sea level and has many major attractions including alpine wilderness, three groves of Giant Sequoia trees; the glacially carved Yosemite Valley with impressive waterfalls, cliffs and unusual rock formations.'

▲ *Statement from the Yosemite National Park*

The main concerns of the park authorities are:

- Traffic congestion in the most popular areas.
- Cars parking illegally, damaging vegetation.
- Increased pollution caused by traffic, noise and litter.
- Disturbance of wildlife (bears, deer).
- Animals are put in danger by people leaving litter which the animals eat.
- Footpath erosion on some trails.
- Development of hotels and other tourism facilities changing the land use.

Visit www.heinemann.co.uk/hotlinks for more information

How can recreational areas be managed?

The following extract is from a travel book . It describes the area leading towards the Great Smoky Mountains National Park in the USA.

'The Great Smoky Mountains National Park covers 500 000 acres in North Carolina in Tennessee. I didn't realise it before I went there, but it is the most popular national park in America, attracting nine million visitors a year, three times as many as in other national parks, and even early on Sunday morning in October it was crowded. The road between Bryson City and Cherokee, at the park's edge, was a straggly collection of motels, junky-looking auto repair shops, trailer courts and barbecue shacks perched on the edge of a glittering stream in a cleft in the mountains. It must have been beautiful once, with dark mountains squeezing in from both sides but now it was just squalid. Cherokee itself was even worse. It is the biggest Indian reservation in the eastern United States and it was packed from one end to the other with souvenir stores selling tawdry Indian trinkets, all of them with big signs on their roofs and sides saying MOCCASINS! INDIAN JEWELRY! TOMAHAWKS! POLISHED GEMSTONES! ITEMS OF EVERY DESCRIPTION! Some of the places had a caged brown bear out front – the Cherokee mascot. At the other stores you could have your photograph taken with a genuine, hung-over Cherokee Indian in war dress for $5, but not many people seemed interested in this and the model Indians sat slumped in chairs looking as listless as the bears. I don't think I had been to a place quite so ugly, and it was jammed with tourists. Then, abruptly, before I could … I was out of Cherokee and in the national park and all the garishness ceased.

▲ Taken from *The Lost Continent – Travels in Small Town America* by Bill Bryson

What are the key points from the extract?

1 National parks attract millions of visitors.

2 National parks are often in areas of spectacular scenery.

3 Where there is little control, areas can become overdeveloped and spoilt.

Case study

Yosemite National Park, USA

The Yosemite National Park Plan has suggested a number of ways that the area could be preserved.

These include:

- Reduce the number of car parks and increase the use of shuttle buses.
- Increase the number of bicycle trails.
- Reduce the number of campsites.
- Direct people away from the most sensitive areas.
- Close damaged areas so that they have time to recover.
- Restrict building development and remove most housing from the Merced Valley (a honeypot area).
- Build a new visitor/education centre.

These measures might protect the area, but:

- Would they reduce visitor numbers?
- How would they affect the people who rely on tourism for employment?

Case study

MEDC

The Lake District National Park

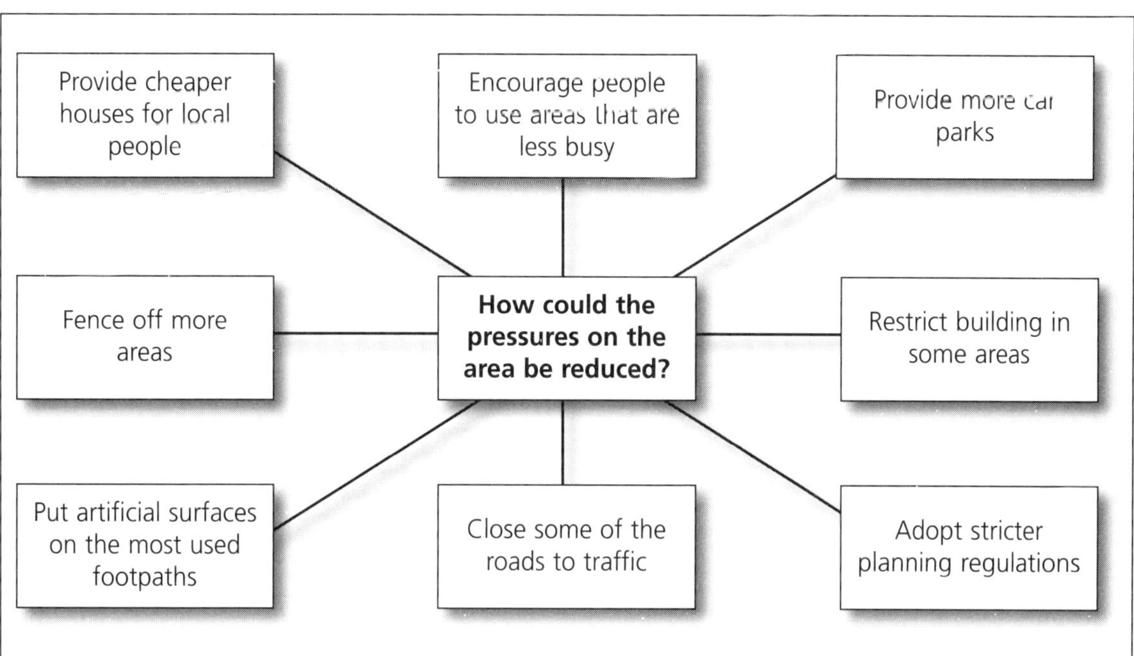

▲ *How could the pressures on the area be reduced?*

Possible advantages of management

- Reduction of pressure in honeypot areas
- Less traffic congestion
- Protection of the most vulnerable areas
- Less unrestricted building.

Possible disadvantages of management

- Reduction in the numbers of visitors
- Fewer tourism related jobs
- Local incomes decline
- Less money for local services and environmental protection.

How can the lakes be managed?

There has been a growth in leisure activities on the lakes in recent years and this has:

- Increased the possibility of water pollution
- Increased the rate of bank-side erosion
- Created a problem of conflict between different groups of users (sailing/fishing/water skiing etc).

Responses to this have been to:

- Ban all water-based activities on some lakes
- Zone lakes so that individual activities can only take place within specified zones.

Lake Windermere is a honeypot site attracting millions of visitors every year. Such is the pressure on Windermere from the many different lake users that a 10-mph speed limit comes into force in 2005. This will enable smaller vessels such as sailing boats and kayaks to enjoy the lake safely, unhampered by the jetskis, water skiers and fast motor boats. However, this decision is a controversial one; many local businesses will lose money. Tourists bring jobs and money into the area but increase traffic congestion and have a significant environmental impact.

Making the grade

Understanding and explaining conflict

Examiners often ask questions about conflict, because it is a good way of testing that candidates understand different points of view.

What is meant by conflict?

Conflict occurs when people have different opinions about a particular issue. It does not mean that one view is right and the other wrong – both opinions can be equally valuable.

The following two views express opinions about the issue of access in national parks:

- An environmentalist. ➔ 'Access to national parks should be restricted in order to protect the landscape.'
- A tourist. ➔ 'Tourists should have completely free access since they spend money in the area – more car parks should be built.'

These two positions represent a 'conflict' since both people want different things from the same landscape.

Conflict questions are often about:

- environmental issues
- tourism issues
- land-use change/building issues
- development issues.

Practice conflict question

The following diagram shows different seasonal activities that might take place in a Scottish mountain environment.

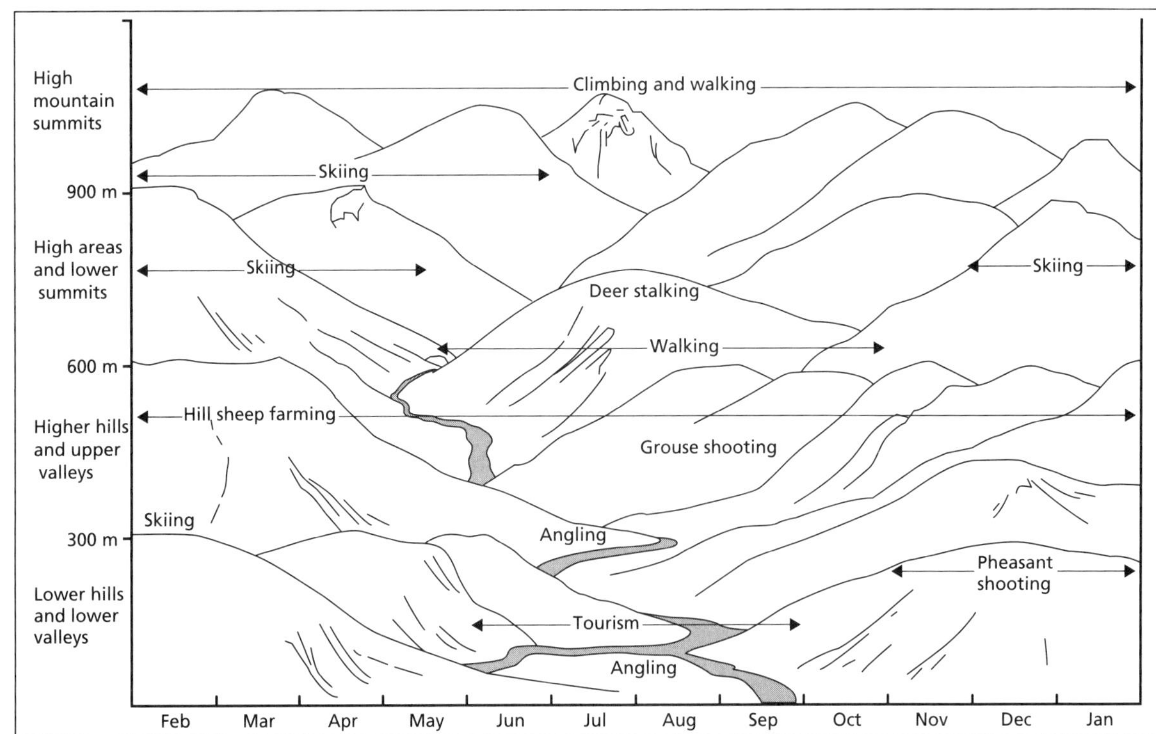

Explain why some of the activities shown on the diagram might conflict with each other.

Exam practice questions

1 Study Figure 1, the sketch section of a coastal area in the UK.

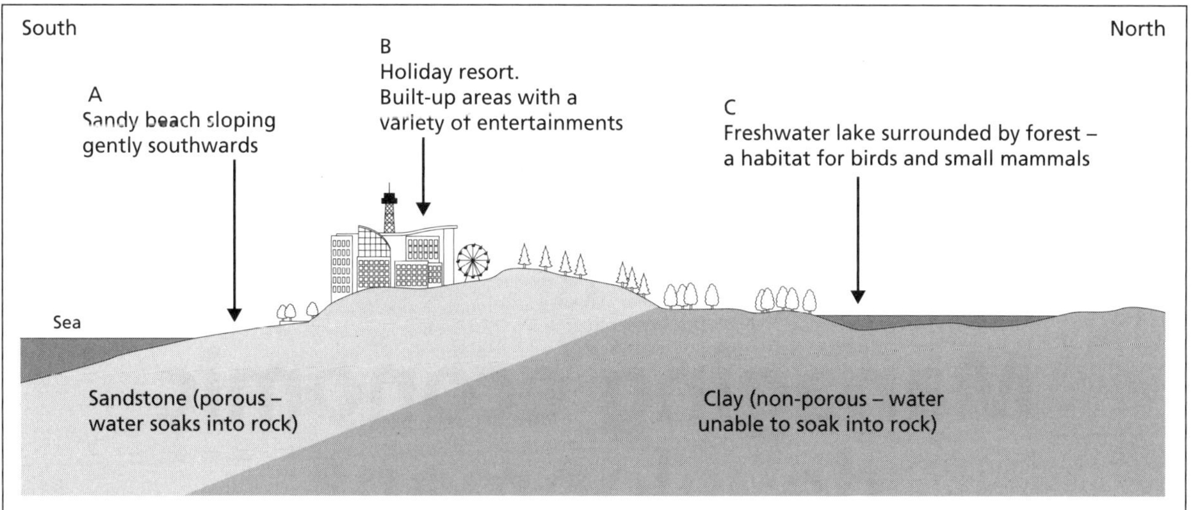

▲ *Figure 1*

Use Figure 1 to answer questions 1(a), (b) and (c).

a) Areas A, B and C are used for leisure activities. Construct and complete the table below by suggesting *one* leisure activity likely to be found in each area.

Area	Leisure activity
A	
B	
C	

(3 marks)

b) Suggest ways in which the *physical environment* might have encouraged the growth of recreation and tourism in each area. (3x2) (6 marks)

c) Explain how the development of tourism might have put pressure on the environment. (6 marks)

2 **a)** State two reasons why national parks were set up in England and Wales. (2 marks)

b) Why has the number of people visiting national parks increased? (4 marks)

3 **a)** Why might conflicts occur in national parks? (4 marks)

b) Using examples you have studied describe how pressures in national parks can be managed. (6 marks)

4 For a landscape you have studied:

a) Explain the formation of one feature of erosion. (4 marks)

b) Explain the formation of one feature of deposition. (4 marks)

Section 3

Managing economic development

Revision checklist

Use this page to check that you have covered everything you need to. If you can't answer any of the questions, go back to the relevant section.

9 Contrasting levels of development	• Which parts of the world are more/less developed? • Why are some parts of the world more developed than others? • How does development affect human and economic conditions? • How does development affect people's quality of life? • How can the gap between MEDCs and LEDCs be reduced? • What are the advantages and disadvantages of different approaches to development?
10 Resource depletion	• What is meant by renewable and non-renewable resources? • Why are some resources running out (depletion)? • What are the effects of resource use on LEDCs? • What are the effects of resource use on MEDCs? • How can the effects of resource use be reduced? • What are the advantages and disadvantages of different methods of managing resource depletion?
11 Managing economic development	• What are the causes of global warming and acid rain? • Why are rainforests being cut down? • How might pollution/deforestation damage the environment? • How might pollution/deforestation affect people? • What are environmental pressure groups? • What are the advantages and disadvantages of different methods of reducing pollution?
12 Tourism and the economy	• How has global tourism grown in the last fifty years? • Why has there been a growth in international tourism? • What are the advantages and disadvantages of tourism in MEDCs? • What are the advantages and disadvantages of tourism in LEDCs? • What is sustainable tourism? • Why is sustainable tourism needed to help preserve the environment?

9 Contrasting levels of development

How can development be measured?

Development refers to the way that a country's economy grows, and how the extra money created can be spent on improving living standards. The following three extracts show that there are enormous differences between countries in terms of wealth. These differences are often related to levels of development.

> **'A child born in the poorest parts of the world will be fortunate to survive the first two years of life and will spend the rest of their short life with problems of food in squalid conditions with few amenities. Opportunities for education or personal development will be limited and little will be passed on to the next generation. A child born in the wealthiest parts of the world will be born with full medical support and will expect to develop into a healthy, well-nourished child. They will be well educated and expect to get a well-paid job, which will allow them to live in a comfortable home with a full range of amenities. Leisure time and holidays will be expected and in the event of illness a doctor or hospital will be available.'**

Adapted text from an Aid poster

> **'If a journalist were to arrive from Mars....his lead story would surely be the discovery that some 1.3 billion people on Earth live in absolute poverty.'**

Jon Snow, television journalist

> **'One in four of the world's population (two-thirds of them women) lives in abject poverty – without access to adequate food, clean water, sanitation, essential healthcare or basic education services. That's 1.3 billion people whose lives are deprived of the opportunity to fulfil their potential.'**

Clare Short, Secretary of State for International Development

How can countries be compared?

Countries are often compared by using the **Gross National Product (GNP)** per capita (person). This is the value of all the goods and services in a country divided by its population, and the resulting figure given in US dollars.

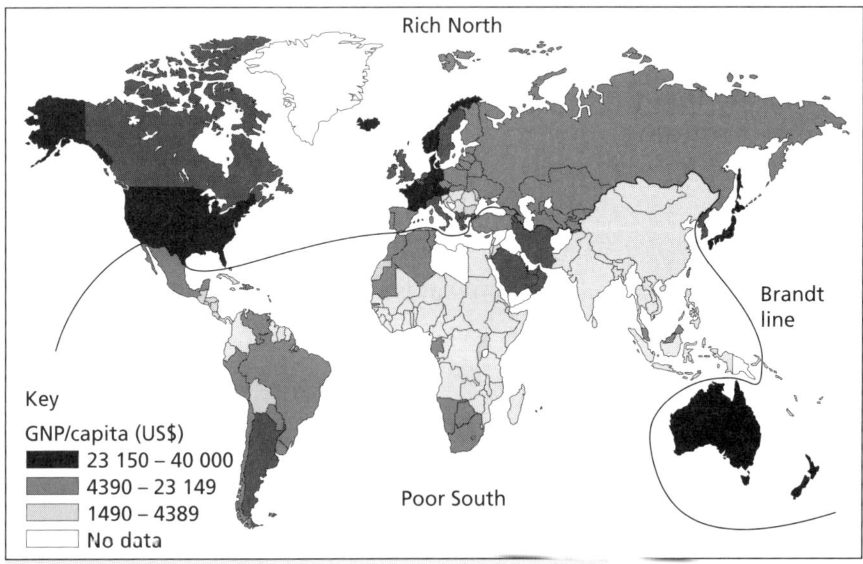

▲ *World development based on GNP/capita (US$)*

What are the limitations of using GNP?

- It is an average and there may be big differences within the country.
- The figures may not be accurate.
- It does not say much about general living conditions.

What other information can be used to compare countries?

To get a more complete picture of relative wealth a range of other statistics can be used, including:

- population data (life expectancy/infant mortality)
- social data (healthcare/education/level of services)
- economic data (income/employment structure/energy use).

Key facts

Employment structure is the proportion of people working in different areas including:

- primary industry – to do with raw materials (farming, mining)
- secondary industry – manufacturing
- tertiary industry – service industry.

Measures of world development, 1997

Status		Country	GNP ($)	Birth rate	Death rate	Life expectancy	Infant mortality	Literacy (%)	People/doctor	Access to safe water (%)	Energy use	Employment structure (%) Primary	Tertiary	Secondary
	High-income countries (MEDCs)	Japan	39 640	10	7	80	4	99	608	85	3856	7	32	58
		USA	26 980	15	9	76	7.3	98	421	85	7819	3	24	70
		UK	18 700	13	11	77	6.2	99	611	96	3772	3	24	70
	Middle-income countries (NICs)	Brazil	3640	22	7	67	48	83	844	73	718	25	25	50
		Mexico	3770	27	5	72	34	89	615	70	1561	23	29	48
	Low-income countries (LEDCs)	Egypt	790	29	8	64	62	51	1316	68	600	40	19	41
		India	340	29	10	59	75	50	2459	29	248	61	14	25
		Kenya	280	38	12	54	62	76	21 970	43	110	78	9	13

Why does a wealth gap exist?

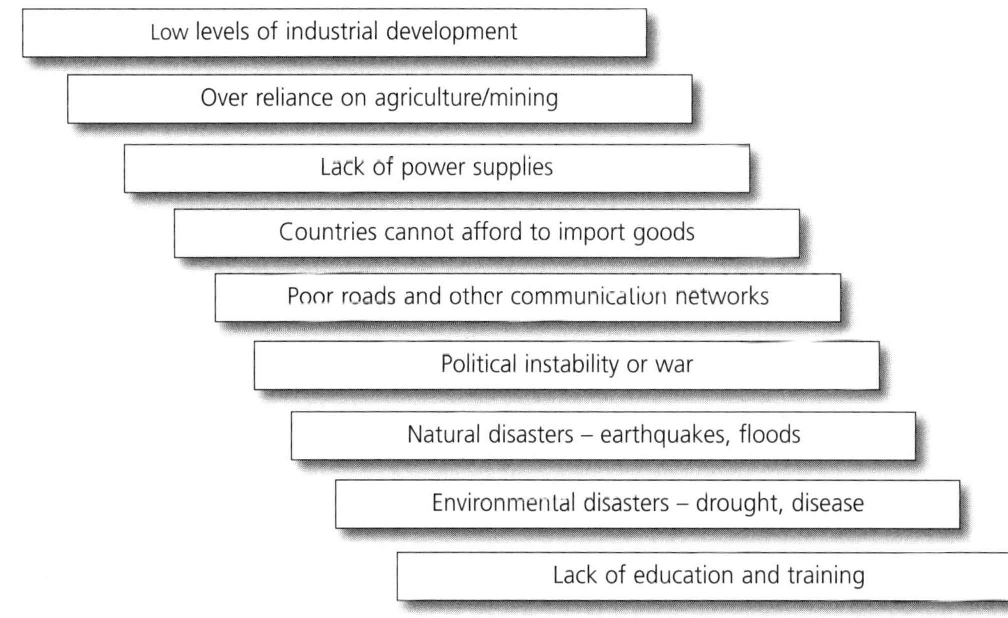

What are the consequences of changing levels of development?

What is meant by the quality of life?

The quality of life is not just about average income, it also includes a number of other factors, for example:

- the availability of education and healthcare
- the quality of housing
- access to services like water and electricity
- the ability to afford a proper diet
- the level of personal safety
- the level of pollution and general environmental conditions.

Database: Kenya and Japan		
	LEDC	MEDC
	Kenya	**Japan**
Birth rate per 1000	38	10
Death rate per 1000	12	7
Infant mortality per 1000	62	4
Life expectancy (years)	54	80
GNP ($)	280	39 640
People working in agriculture (%)	75	7
Urban population (%)	27	78
Adult literacy (%)	76	99
People per doctor	21 970	608
Access to safe water (%)	43	85
Access to sanitation (%)	43	85
Cars per 1000 people	14	520
Telephones per 1000 people	9	487
Energy use (kg oil per person)	110	3856

▶ *A database showing measures of development for Kenya (LEDC) and Japan (MEDC). As a country develops it has the opportunity to spend more money on services.*

What is the Human Development Index?

The Human Development Index is a measure of social welfare, because it takes into account both social and economic factors. It uses the following data to construct an index:

- life expectancy
- school enrolment and attainment (literacy rates/years in school)
- the 'real' GNP per person – not just the amount of money but what it will actually buy in that country.

▼ *Example of the HDI*

Country	Life expectancy	Education	Real GNP	HDI	Conclusion
Canada	.90	.99	.96	.96	Very highly developed country
Sierra Leone	.14	.30	.17	.17	Very poor level of development

Each of these three variables is ranked from 0 to 1, with the poorest at 0 and the best at 1. So a country with very high life expectancy will have a figure close to 1. The HDI is the average of the three scores: the higher the number, the more economically and socially developed the country.

Top five countries, 1997		Bottom five countries, 1997	
Canada	.960	Mali	.229
France	.946	Burkina Faso	.221
Norway	.943	Niger	.206
United States	.942	Rwanda	.187
Iceland	.942	Sierra Leone	.176
UK	.92	World average	.76

▶ *The top and bottom five countries using the HDI, plus the United Kingdom (UK)*

Case study

LEDC

Industrial development in south-east Brazil

South-east Brazil is the most developed part of the country and consequently has the highest living standards.

What are the reasons for development?

- The area has a long history of agricultural development.
- A range of raw materials, including iron ore, gold and diamonds are found locally.
- There are large ports, including Rio de Janeiro, ideal for trade.
- There is a good road and rail network.
- Power can be generated from fast-flowing rivers.
- The area has a broad range of industries (car manufacture/ food processing/ tourism etc).
- Lots of multinational companies are found in the area (Ford/ VW/ Fiat).

What are the benefits of development?

- Local incomes are twice the national average.
- There are more opportunities for work.
- Better education/ training is available.
- People can afford a slightly better standard of living.

What are the problems of development?

- Overcrowding and the development of slums as people move to the industrial cities.
- Increasing traffic congestion and pollution.
- Increasing environmental problems.
- People working long hours for low wages.

Case study

NIC

Oil-rich countries – the Middle East

Oil is one of the world's most important sources of energy and at present most countries could not manage without it. A small number of countries in the Middle East have been able to sell large amounts of oil in recent years because they produce far more than they need.

The wealth produced through selling oil has enabled some of these countries to develop rapidly, building new cities, communication networks, and large areas of housing with schools and hospitals.

Few countries have changed as much as Kuwait and Saudi Arabia in the last 50 years. Kuwait was described as 'a small and sleepy mud-walled trading and fishing port' before the discovery of oil, while in the 1950s most of Saudi Arabia's people were desert nomads. Both of these countries have developed major oil-refining and petrochemical industries and today they have highly developed economic and social facilities. Most of the population live in modern cities, their children go to school, and living standards are high. However, some people have regrets about such rapid development and feel that it has put pressure on traditional ways of life and values, and increased the gap between rich and poor.

		Saudi Arabia	Kuwait
Life expectancy	1981	60	71
	1995	71	76
Literacy rate (%)	1981	25	61
	1995	60	77
People/doctor	1981	1819	589
	1995	749	N/A
GNP ($)	1995	7040	17 390
Infant mortality	1995	29	13
Access to sanitation	1995	86%	94% (est.)
Access to safe water	1995	93%	98% (est)
N/A = not available			

▲ *Some of the differences between 1981 and 1995 in Saudi Arabia and Kuwait*

How can the gap between MEDCs and LEDCs be reduced?

Multinational investment

A multinational or transnational company is one which operates in a number of countries. The headquarters is usually in the developed world and branch factories are found in many developing countries. These factories provide much needed work and incomes in LEDCs but are often seen as exploiting cheap labour. The biggest multinational companies are some of the car and oil companies and include:

- General Motors
- Ford
- Toyota
- Shell Energy
- BP Energy.
- Exxon Energy.

Advantages of multinationals (to LEDCs)

- They provide work and regular incomes.
- They train local people and improve skill levels.
- They can lead to the development of other industry.
- They bring money into the country.

Disadvantages of multinationals (to LEDCs)

- Wages are lower than in MEDCs.
- Working conditions can be poor.
- Environmental management is often poor.
- Major profits go back to MEDCs.

The development of tourism

The following article shows how tourism has grown in LEDCs:

> 'There are a large number of popular places for tourists to visit in LEDCs. Some have been popular for many years, for example safari holidays in Kenya and historical tours to Cairo (Egypt). More recently the coastal regions of Venezuela and western India have become popular. If you want sand, sea and sun, the Caribbean or Goa (India) may suit you. For a more historical or cultural holiday, Cairo or China might be interesting. Those who want more adventure might choose mountain trekking in the Himalayas or even a river trip in the Amazon rainforest.'

▲ *An interview with a travel agent*

Advantages of tourism (to LEDCs)

- It can bring in a lot of money.
- It can create many jobs.
- It can help the development of a range of industries (building/farming).
- It can help develop transport systems.

Disadvantages of tourism (to LEDCs)

- Wages are often low.
- It can cause conflict with local people.
- Building large holiday resorts can damage the environment.
- A large number of visitors can cause a lot of pollution.

Development projects

The aim of a development project is to improve living standards. Development projects can vary in scale from multi-million dollar projects such as the Three Gorges Dam Scheme (China) or the Aswan Dam Scheme (Egypt) to small-scale aid projects affecting local communities. Small-scale projects are often seen as more appropriate and sustainable, often using intermediate technology.

Definitions

Appropriate technology Technology that is suited to the needs of the country.
Intermediate technology Matching the level of technology to the needs and skills of local people.
Sustainable development Improving living standards without damaging the environment or making anyone worse off.

Case study

Intermediate Technology – a small-scale development project

LEDC

Intermediate Technology (IT) is an international development organization which works with small-scale producers in Africa, Asia and South America. IT helps people to develop and use skills and technologies which can give them more control over their lives and which contribute to locally based sustainable development.

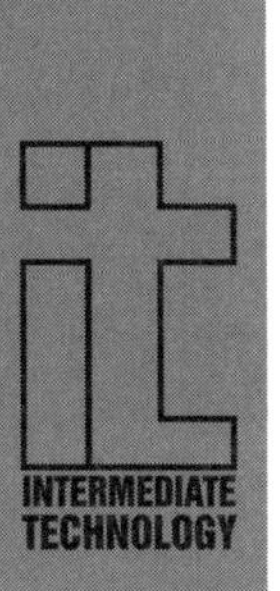

The organization was founded in 1966 with the aim that you should "find out what people are doing, and then help them to do it better". IT's development work is based on this idea. IT's main focus countries are: Peru, Kenya, Sudan, Zimbabwe, Bangladesh and Sri Lanka. It is also active in India and Nepal. Many of the world's poorest people earn their living from small-scale enterprise in areas such as farming, food processing and blacksmithing. IT's intervention enables people to combine existing skills and knowledge of appropriate technology with scientific and technological knowledge from the wider world without harming local culture and the environment.

▲ *Extract from www.globaleye.org.uk* published by *Worldaware*

Reducing debt

Many poor countries spend a lot of valuable money simply paying off interest on debts. If countries could reduce these debts, they could spend more on reducing poverty and developing basic services.

Changing the terms of trade

Trade between MEDCs and LEDCs often favours MEDCs because:

- MEDCs protect their markets and do not always allow goods in from LEDCs.
- LEDCs export mainly primary goods which are low in price.
- The price of raw materials is usually determined in the MEDCs.
- There is a significant gap in price between the basic raw material and the finished product and this difference is often earned by MEDCs.

If LEDCs could earn more through trade they would be able to spend more on economic and social development.

Case study

Uganda

LEDC

The following example looks at how the World Bank has helped Uganda reduce international debts:

In May 2000, the World Bank's IDA (International Development Agency) announced that Uganda would receive debt relief amounting to a total of almost $2 billion. Uganda qualified for debt relief because of its progress in reducing poverty and implementing economic reform. The debt relief will enable more public expenditure on poverty reduction. Debt relief will be given to the Uganda Poverty Action Fund (PAF), for anti-poverty programmes.
Two examples of Uganda's progress are as follows:

- The share of the population living in poverty has declined to 44 per cent in 1996/97, from 56 per cent in 1992/93.
- The number of children enrolled in primary schools has risen to 6.5 million children in March 1999 from 2.3 million in December 1996.

▲ *Extract from* World Poverty: responding to the challenge, *available at www.worldaware.org.uk – Worldaware*

Making the grade

Using data in examination questions

Examiners often use statistical data as part of a question.

It can be used to test:

- skills – identification of trends/ presentation of data
- understanding – using the data to explain certain factors
- knowledge – about the data itself
  – as a prompt to discuss different places.

The key to success is:

- to make sure all data use and presentation is accurate
- to use the data (quote from it) to help make specific points.

Practice data question

Study the following information which shows development data for different countries.

	Country	GNP ($)	Life expectancy	Infant mortality	People/doctor
High-income countries (MEDCs)	Japan	39 640	80	4	608
	USA	26 980	76	7.3	421
	UK	18 700	77	6.2	611
Middle-income countries (NICs)	Brazil	3640	67	48	844
	Mexico	3770	72	34	615
Low-income countries (LEDCs)	Egypt	790	64	62	1316
	India	340	59	75	2459
	Kenya	280	54	62	21 970

Definitions

GNP ($) Gross National Product
Life expectancy How long a person is expected to live at the time of birth
Infant mortality Number of deaths per 1000 live births
People/doctor Number of people for each doctor

▲ *Figure 1 Development data (1997)*

a) Which country:
  i) has the highest GNP ($)?
  ii) has the lowest life expectancy? (2 marks)

b) Describe and explain the relationship between GNP and life expectancy. (4 marks)

c) Why is GNP not always a good measure of development? (4 marks)

d) Why is infant mortality a useful measure of living standards? (6 marks)

Exam practice questions

1 Study Figure 1, which gives information about living standards in six countries.

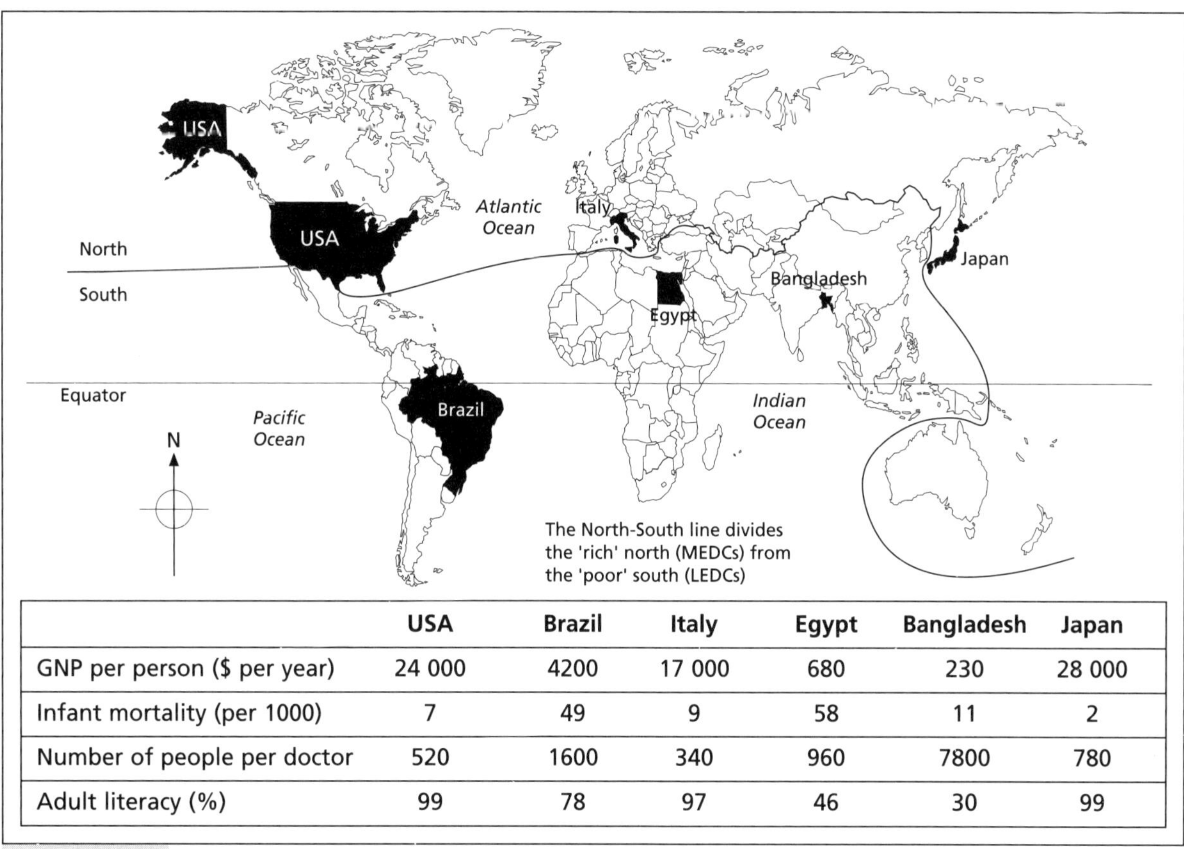

	USA	Brazil	Italy	Egypt	Bangladesh	Japan
GNP per person ($ per year)	24 000	4200	17 000	680	230	28 000
Infant mortality (per 1000)	7	49	9	58	11	2
Number of people per doctor	520	1600	340	960	7800	780
Adult literacy (%)	99	78	97	46	30	99

▲ *Figure 1*

Use Figure 1 to answer questions 1(a) and (b).

1 a) Which country:
(i) Has the highest income?
(ii) Has the highest number of people per doctor?
(iii) Has the lowest infant mortality? (3 marks)

b) Explain why 'number of people per doctor' and 'adult literacy' are useful indicators of economic development. (6 marks)

c) When comparing levels of development, the world is often divided into MEDCs and LEDCs.
Why might this only give a simple picture of global differences? (4 marks)

2 Why are some countries richer than others? (4 marks)

3 Using examples you have studied, describe the way that living standards in LEDCs can be improved. (6 marks)

10 Resource depletion

Why are some non-renewable resources being used up so rapidly?

The rate at which we consume non-renewable resources is increasing. Fossil fuels, such as coal, oil and gas, are made from plants and animal remains over millions of years (1 year's energy use of fossil fuels took 1 million years to make).

Key facts

- A resource is anything that we can use to meet our needs.
- A non- renewable resource, such as coal, once used cannot be replaced.

Definitions

Non-renewable but recyclable resources Those resources that can be reused, such as aluminium (from bauxite). Half the cans in the world are recycled

Renewable resources but which can be depleted Those resources that will replenish themselves naturally but only if not over used or contaminated, such as fish or trees

Naturally renewable resources Those resources that are with us all the time and over which we have no control, such as the sun and wind

Reserve A non-renewable resource, such as coal or oil, which exists in a finite quantity which can be exploited

OPEC (Organization of Petroleum Exporting Countries) The majority group of oil producers, which together coordinate production and prices

Fossil Fuels Fuels consisting of hydrocarbons laid down in geological times, for example coal and oil

Why do we use non-renewable resources?	**How long will they last?**
Coal – the most-used fuel for generating electricity globally, 37%. There is a big trade in coal and some MEDCs and LEDCs rely on it to produce nearly all their electricity.	200–300 years depending on where and how it is mined.
Oil – used to generate about 9% of electricity and 40% of world energy; 20 countries produce 95% of the world oil.	40–45 years at present rate of consumption (OPEC reserves, 80 years)
Gas – natural gas is produced from most oil fields and is used for 16% of world electricity production.	50–65 years at present consumption
Minerals – such as iron, copper, lead, zinc, potash etc are essential to our daily lives in products as diverse as drink cans, tools and bridges.	Some can be recycled indefinitely but some are used once and thrown away.
Who uses non-renewable resources?	**Who needs them?**
MEDCs use most globally, the USA being the biggest user; it produces its own and also imports non-renewable resources. Developing LEDCs, such as India, depend on coal and half of LEDCs use oil for 75% of their commercial energy needs.	Most of world transport uses fossil fuels and all MEDCs use non-renewable resources. The export of non-renewable resources is an important source of income for LEDCs and many depend on fossil fuels for energy.

Are we depleting renewable resources?

Forests

Estimates are that 40 per cent of the Amazon rainforest has been consumed since 1960 and at the present rate it could all be used within 40 years. Logging has destroyed 90 per cent of the USA temperate forest. More timber is used in the world than is renewed.

Fish stocks

Ocean fish stocks are in danger of depletion from over fishing. It is said that cod face total depletion in the North Sea because of over fishing. Coastal fisheries around Asia and East and West Africa, which provide valuable protein, are also in danger because of over fishing and, in places, development of the coastline endangers fish because of pollution.

Water

The majority of people in the world do not have easy access to clean water and yet MEDCs 'waste' huge quantities in industry and everyday living. Water can be contaminated so that it ceases to be a usable resource.

Fertile soil

Food production and agriculture globally depend on fertile soil. Soil takes a long time to develop but is eroded by wind or water if left without protection. Soil in cleared Amazon areas rapidly loses its fertility.

Case study

Why is Brazil's rainforest being cleared?

The Brazil rainforest is the largest area of Equatorial rainforest left in the world but it is being reduced in size every year as forest is cleared. The amount being cleared is increasing each year for a number of reasons.

- **Farming** Since the 1970s free land has been given to settlers but the subsistence farming is poor and when the rainforest is cleared the soil is unprotected from heavy rain and it loses nutrients. Dense rainforest becomes poor land, growing only poor crops.
- **Cattle ranches** Transnational corporations producing beef (mostly for export) have cleared large areas for cattle ranching.
- **Logging** Much clearing is the result of logging for hardwoods for use in SE Brazil and for export.
- **Mining** The largest global iron ore deposit is being developed in a huge open-cast mine at Grand Carajas in Para state (again, mostly for export – it accounts for 8 per cent of global iron ore). Mining the rich deposits of iron, bauxite and gold from open-cast mines is destroying large areas of forest but the development that comes with it also results in forest loss.
- **HEP** Power comes from hydro-electricity generated at dams blocking huge lakes created by flooding the forest. The Tucurui HEP station was built on the River Tocantins to power the Carajas development; the relatively shallow lake covered a large area of forest.
- **Population growth** The population of the area has increased by 30 million since the 1960s. Growing towns and settlements support the commercial developments, resulting in yet more forest loss.

◀ *Burning the forest*

What are the effects of shortages of resources?

Resource depletion will affect people, economies and environments in different ways. The impacts will differ between **producers** and **consumers** and **MEDCs** and **LEDCs**.

Who uses most resources?

The more developed a country the more resources are consumed. MEDCs use most, with the USA using more than any other country. Fossil fuels are essential to MEDC economies now. Most people in the USA use a car, and most cities are designed around their use, particularly in places such as Los Angeles (about 100 km across), so large quantities of petrol are used.

Who makes money from resource use?

The producer of, for example, oil or bauxite makes some money from selling the raw material and often these producer countries are LEDCs. More money is made when that raw material is turned into a product, such as petrol or aluminium. This generally occurs in an MEDC.

What impacts might resource depletion have on LEDCs and MEDCs?

LEDCs

- Pollution levels are high in, for example Nigeria in West Africa and in Siberia, Russia where oil extraction has polluted the landscape. The depletion of oil reserves would have a positive effect on the environment and people's health, but there would also be a negative effect due to the loss of jobs.
- The economy of a country dependent on oil will suffer when oil begins to run out. Venezuela, South America, exports a lot of oil and gas; it was the third biggest OPEC exporter of oil in 2002. The economy will suffer greatly with the loss of income when the reserves are depleted. The effect is similar in any country that relies for income on exporting one product. If the global price for that resource falls, so will the quality of life in a producer country. The world price of tin dropped by 66 per cent in the late 1980s and the economy of Bolivia, South America, which depended on the tin export, lost a lot of money and suffered badly. Many LEDCs are dependent on the export of one primary product, ranging from iron ore to sugar, and they are therefore very vulnerable to global changing prices.
- LEDCs need resources to develop. Countries such as South Africa, China and India (2.5 billion people) depend on coal for over 80 per cent of their energy production.
- The depletion of resources such as fish affects both the fishermen who depend on it for their livelihoods as well as the people who depend on it for their main source of protein. It also damages the environment by changing the ecology.
- Shortages of soil, food and water lead to malnutrition and expensive food has to be imported which many people cannot afford to buy.
- LEDCs cannot afford the research and development to overcome these shortages that are due to resource depletion.

MEDCs

- The decline of oil/gas will reduce the income in the United Kingdom, Norway and other producing countries, such as Saudi Arabia.
- Oil price rises increase the cost of petroleum and so the cost of travel and the transport of goods as well as all petroleum-based products rise as well.
- The high standard of living in MEDCs depends on resource use, so as resources and goods become more expensive the standard of living may fall.
- TNCs (Trans National Corporations) will want to keep using shortage resources, such as oil, to maintain a profit.
- MEDCs can afford to develop alternative power supplies (such as wind power) and to make recycling more effective.

Case study

MEDC

The decline of coal mining in the United Kingdom

As finite fossil fuels run out and the cost of extraction becomes greater, mines, quarries, oil and gas fields are closed. Early North Sea gas fields have been abandoned. During the 1990s production of coal more than halved with the closure of 48 collieries. Other causes of the closures included the use of imported coal, gas instead of coal in power stations and the growth of alternative energies. Using gas also depletes a fossil fuel and imported coal is mostly from vast open-cast mines, for example, in Australia, which are environmentally damaging.

South Yorkshire is one of the poorest parts of the EU and qualifies for EU and UK funding to aid regeneration after the decline of coal mining. Former mining communities still suffer social and economic problems. Collieries in rural areas had provided most of the work and money in the villages. When they closed unemployment levels were high. The ex-mining areas were poor, with high levels of deprivation and probably the lowest disposable incomes in the UK. Health was poor, life expectancy lower than the rest of the UK and many young people had to leave the area to find work. Open-cast mining can provide employment in these areas but it does damage the environment.

Case study

LEDC

What are the effects of deforestation in Brazil?

The Brazilian rainforest is the largest remaining rainforest in the world. Its destruction not only means that Brazil suffers from a loss of resources, it also has a global impact on climate and biodiversity. Some of the effects are as follows:

- Loss of tree canopy results in soil erosion and loss of soil fertility
- Changes in ecosystem cause an increase in droughts
- Decrease of biodiversity – one result is the loss of plants used in medicines
- Loss of global forest means less forest to absorb CO_2, while forest burning increases CO_2
- Loss of hardwood trees
- Loss of Amerindian tribes and cultures: Amerindians reduced from 6 million to 200 000

▶ *Large-scale destruction of the forest*

How might sustainable development be useful as resources run out?

Sustainable development is defined as 'development that meets the needs of the present without compromising the ability of future generations to meet their own needs'. Anything we do today should not damage the environment or deplete resources to such an extent that future generations are unable to live in the same way.

How can we make more appropriate use of resources?

- **Recycling** – cuts waste disposal costs, saves energy, conserves resources, creates jobs, keeps streets clean. Recycling provides money and informal work in many LEDCs and is very important for people with a poor quality of life. Recycling in MEDCs raises awareness of the need to conserve resources. Recycling is good for the environment but the cost is high. Governments and the EU require companies to meet recycling targets. In the UK 46 per cent of material from drinks cans is recovered but in Germany it is 80 per cent.
- **Appropriate technology** – an efficient use of resources, for example small-scale solar power cookers instead of fuelwood in LEDCs. MEDCs have the money and technology to develop a range of alternatives from houses built from straw bales to wind energy or electric cars.
- **Forests** – a timber, ecological and tourist resource, but only if the forest is sustainably managed. 835 million visitor days are spent in USA temperate forests; tourism, which generates 38 times more money than logging, may be a more appropriate use of the forest. Companies, such as B & Q in the UK, can influence forest depletion through their buying policy, which states 'all our wood or paper products come either from proven, well managed forests or recycled material'.
- **Fish** – fish stocks that provide food through inshore or deep sea fishing can be protected by quotas, which prevent countries from depleting the fish stock below replacement level. Controls placed on North Sea fishing to restrict catches and preserve fish stock may prevent depletion of supplies.

Key facts

- 21 per cent of energy produced globally is from renewable resources and this proportion could be increased in future. About 3 per cent of UK energy is from renewable sources with a target of 5 per cent set for 2005.
- Sustainable development could improve the quality of life for people in LEDCs and MEDCs, reducing ill health as a result of air pollution, vehicle emissions, mining etc. by using alternative resources and energy supplies
- Sustainable development of soil, water, fish, forests and power sources could help the economies of LEDCs. MEDCs could benefit from a reduction in their consumption and need to import resources.
- The global environment would be enhanced and protected if present damaging methods of resource extraction and use were changed.
- Sustainable development can be encouraged (for example recycling), enforced through government regulations and controls (on emissions, energy use etc.) and through global agreements (Agenda 21, Rio Conference 1992) and by persuasion by groups such as Friends of the Earth, Greenpeace, Sierra Club.

Are there alternative ways to produce energy?

Type of energy	How is it used?	Advantages	Disadvantages
Hydro-Electric Power	Produces 7% of commercial energy, large scale (Aswan Dam, Egypt) or small scale, (Norway)	Little pollution when running; cheap; lakes can be used for recreation; can help control floods	Dams expensive to build, flood lots of land; can create methane from rotting vegetation
Wind	Produces 0.2% of UK energy in windy, exposed places	Running costs low; no air pollution; provides income for farmers; most effective in strong winds, usually winter	Expensive to build and maintain; noisy, unsightly; very large numbers needed (30 turbines produce power for only 50 000 homes)
Solar	Commonly used on small scale, e.g. parking metres; could be effective in LEDCs with long hours of constant sunshine	Very good for small scale uses, alternative and appropriate technology for LEDCs; no pollution	Expensive to set up, especially on large scale; limited locations
Biomass (non fossil organic material which has a chemical energy content)	Biomass derived fuels can be produced from fermented organic material, e.g. sugar alcohol for vehicles (Brazil), or it can be burnt in power stations	Can be grown; renewable; absorbs greenhouse gases; can make use of poor land	Large growing area needed; specialist equipment necessary; burning gives off greenhouse gases
Biogas	Methane from rotting animal dung can be used for energy	Especially useful for LEDCs	Dung cannot be used for fertilizer if used for biogas
Geothermal	Heat, as steam, from the Earth can be used to generate electricity (Iceland)	Renewable, reliable, non-polluting	Limited locations with possible danger of earthquakes, eruptions and sulphur; expensive to build and maintain
Wave	Potential for harnessing the surface energy in waves in windy places; limited development so far	Masses of free energy in waves	Expensive; equipment to survive severe weather still being developed
Nuclear	Countries such as France which lack fossil fuels increasingly use this power	Can be seen as clean, little air pollution, small quantity raw material, government support, lowish running costs	High costs of decommissioning; some water pollution; radioactive waste difficult to dispose of; accident fears
Tidal	Tidal range used in River Rance, France, where turbines in a dam are turned by the incoming tide and again as the tide goes out; potential across River Severn in UK for a barrage and turbines	Unlimited supply, no pollution	Expensive to build; floods estuaries

Making the grade

Command words

Command words are the words in the question that tell you what to do. The mark scheme will reflect these command words and if you do not do what you are asked to do you will not be awarded many marks.

- **Name, state, give** Asks you to give a brief answer to a question, such as 'give the 6 figure reference.....' These questions may carry one or two marks.
- **What is at…?** What is shown…? Also require a simple answer.
- **Annotate** Asks you to add notes to a map or diagram.
- **Why** Asks you to show your understanding, such as in 'why do some countries have high death rates?' There may be varying ways in which information about death rates can be looked at.
- **Describe** One of the most widely used command words that asks you to give a picture of something. There will be indicators as to what to describe, such as 'describe the main features of this development' or 'describe the attractions of a honeypot site'. The account should be factual. 'Describe the changes in…' may be used in relation to a graph so you will use words reflecting change such as rapidly or steeply as well as using the figures from the graph.
- **Explain** Asks you to state why something occurs. This questioning tests your ability to know or understand why something happens. Answers may be several lines in length with higher marks.
- **Describe and explain** Asks you to give a picture and the reasons why that picture occurs, for example 'describe and explain the pattern of roads shown on the map'.
- **Suggest reasons for** Allows you to put forward several reasons in explanation. There may be varying ways in which a change or issue may be explained in questions such as 'suggest reasons why tourists may be attracted to this area'. This may be a more frequent type of questioning than 'describe and explain'.
- **Give your views** Asks you to state what you think about an issue. Logical reasoning should support your answer.

Do remember the specification is issue based and there are these commands in the specification. **Investigate** the background to the issues, **understand** the impacts and consequences and **consider** alternative strategies for more effective management of issues.

Exam practice questions

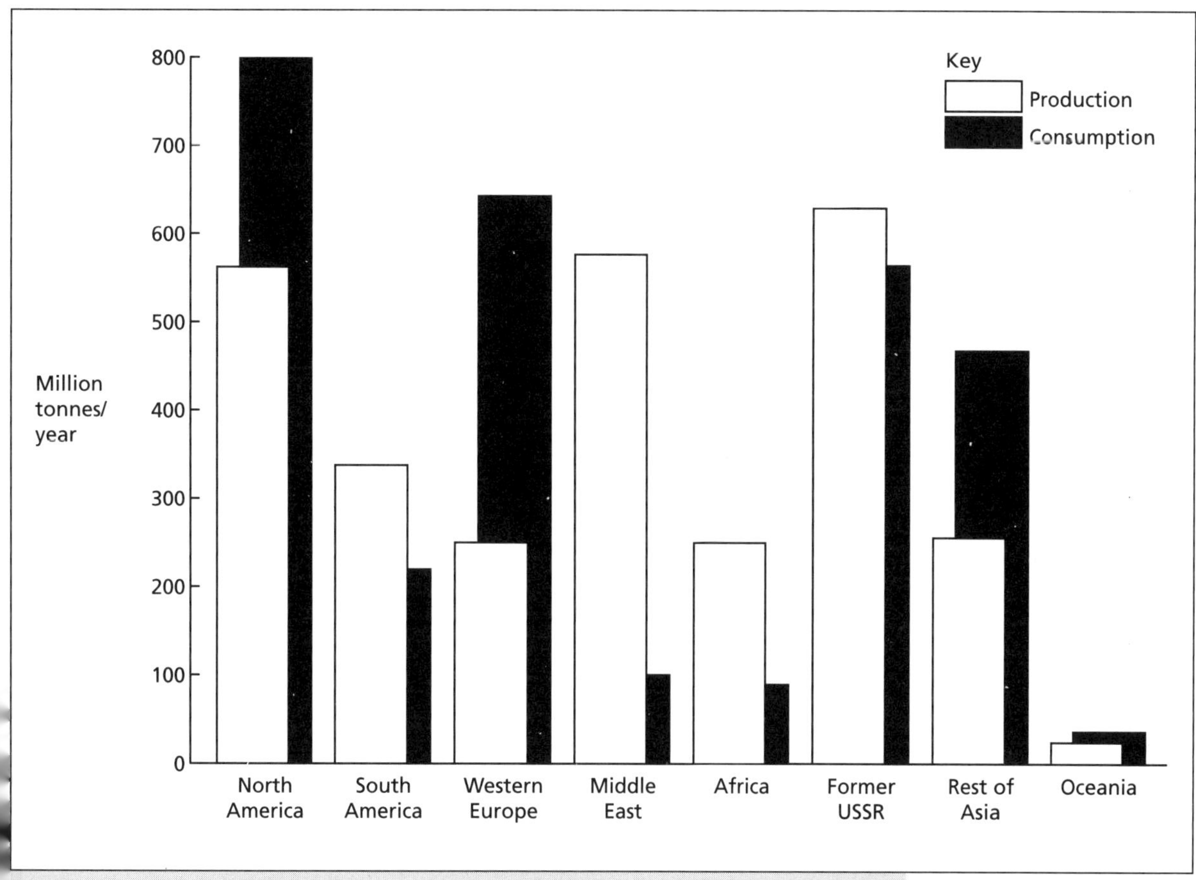

▲ *Figure 1 Production and consumption of oil in different parts of the world.*

1 a) Study Figure 1 and state which part of the world
 i) produces the most oil?
 ii) consumes most oil
 iii) has the biggest differences between production and consumption? (3 marks)

b) Give two reasons why some areas use more oil than others. (2 marks)

2

Resource	Renewable	Non-renewable
Coal		✔
Timber	✔	
	✔	
		✔

◀ *Figure 2*

a) Complete Figure 2 by adding one renewable and one non-renewable resource. The first two have been done for you. (2 marks)

b) Name a renewable resource that can be depleted. (1 mark)

c) Suggest two ways in which forests may be used as a resource. (4 marks)

3 Using examples, describe how resource extraction has caused environmental damage. (6 marks)

4 Suggest ways in which the use of either recycling or appropriate technology can reduce resource consumption. (6 marks)

11 Managing economic development

What global environmental problems are being caused by economic development?

Key facts

- For two centuries economic development has been taking place and so has environmental damage.
- Energy, vital for development, has been obtained by burning fossil fuels and this has been the cause of most air pollution and contributed to global warming.
- Industrial processes and accidents have led to pollution of land, sea and air.
- People in LEDCs and MEDCs are affected by global environmental problems.

Definitions

Ozone layer A concentration of ozone in a layer 10–15 km above sea level which shields the Earth from most of the harmful ultra violet radiation from the sun. See also www.heineman.co.uk/hotlinks for more information.

What sort of environmental problems are global?

Most environmental problems have a global affect and require international agreements to control them. For example, polluted water in the North Sea from surrounding industrialized countries spreads pollution further into the oceans.

Who is affected?

Everybody in the world is affected in some way by global warming and millions will experience sea level rises. Countries in the path of prevailing winds from industrial locations may be affected by acid rain (e.g. Scandinavia). The thinning ozone layer holes may leave millions of people open to skin and eye damage (e.g. North West Europe). People in urban areas or near industrial factories may suffer air or water pollution that damages their health (e.g. Cubatao, Brazil; Tokyo, Japan).

What are the major global environmental problems?

- **Global warming** The Earth is getting warmer and the global climate is changing. The speed of change is accelerating. In the twentieth century the climate warmed by about 0.6°C but this could increase by 2–4°C by 2050. Global warming is largely a result of the increase of carbon dioxide by 15 per cent in the atmosphere over the last 100 years. Burning fossil fuels in power stations, industry and vehicles has contributed most CO_2 – the result of economic development.
- **Acid rain** Acid rain occurs when sulphur dioxides and nitrogen oxides combine in the atmosphere with water vapour, sunlight and oxygen to produce dilute sulphuric and nitric acid. Buildings, trees, vegetation and people over a wide area are affected. Acid rain is mostly caused by burning fossil fuels for power generation (as in the UK, USA), older industrial plants (especially metal production, Eastern European countries) and exhaust fumes from motor vehicles (urban areas in LEDCs and MEDCs, e.g. Mexico City).
- **Ozone depletion** Ozone depletion takes place when the rate at which the layer is destroyed is greater than the rate at which it is formed. 'Holes' appear in the layer over the Arctic, the Antarctic and other parts of the world. Chemicals used in our daily lives have depleted the ozone in the atmosphere and allowed UV radiation to reach the Earth's surface causing damage to people, animals and plants.

What are the major causes of environmental problems?

1 **Pollutants** called greenhouse gases trap heat around the Earth, raising the global temperature and contributing to global warming.

2 **Deforestation** is the globally widespread depletion of forests for commercial logging or land clearance. The easiest way to clear forests is by burning which only adds more CO_2 to the atmosphere. At the same time the number of trees absorbing CO_2 is reduced. In 1998, for example, there were 15 000 forest burning fires in Nicaragua. Atmospheric pollution of SE Asia often happens during annual forest and land clearance fires in Indonesia (see page 93 about deforestation in Brazil).

3 **Accidents**. Accidents with industrial processes (e.g. Bhopal, India), power generation (e.g. radioactive discharges from Sellafield, UK) and fossil fuel transport (e.g. the Exxon Valdez oil tanker accident, Alaska) can have international impacts.

Pollutants include:

- **Carbon dioxide** from burning fossil fuels in power stations, factories, homes and vehicles provides nearly 75 per cent of greenhouse gases. As countries develop, the amount of power consumed increases as does the number of vehicles, and so the use of fossil fuels rises.
- **CFCs (chloroflurocarbons)** make up approximately 13 per cent of greenhouse gases and they come from plastics, foam, refrigerators and aerosol cans. CFCs last for fifty years in the atmosphere so, although they have been banned in aerosols and fridges are being discarded very carefully now, the effects will last for some time. CFCs deplete the ozone layer.
- **Nitrous Oxide** (about 5 per cent of greenhouse gases) comes from a variety of sources including cars, power stations and fertilizers sprayed onto the ground.
- **Methane** (about 10 per cent of greenhouse gases) is released from agriculture (rice fields), animals (slurry pits and the animals themselves, mostly cows and sheep) and waste disposal sites (particularly in MEDCs).

Case study

The Prestige oil tanker accident, November 2002

On Wednesday 13 November 2002 the oil tanker the Prestige encountered violent storms off the Galician coast of Spain and started to leak oil. It was carrying more than 75 000 tonnes of fuel oil which made the accident potentially one of the worst in the world. Oil slicks spread towards the shore and, within a week, had polluted 400 km of coastline. It was described as 'an environmental catastrophe'. Many people in the area depend on primary employment in the fishing industry but fishing and shellfish production were banned leaving many people with no income. Those in charge were confused as to how to manage the disaster and it was three days before anti-pollution barriers were available. Local people came down to the beaches to try to clear the thick, sticky oil. Eventually the boat was towed out to deep water, trailing more oil slicks and it sank with 70 000 tonnes of oil still on board. It was hoped that the thick oil would solidify, stay in the tanker and not be a long-term threat but by 30 November a slick of 11 000 tonnes (twice the size of the first spill) approached the newly cleaned coast. Ships from six nations helped with the clean up. Local people demanded a European global plan to combat accidents in the busy international shipping lane.

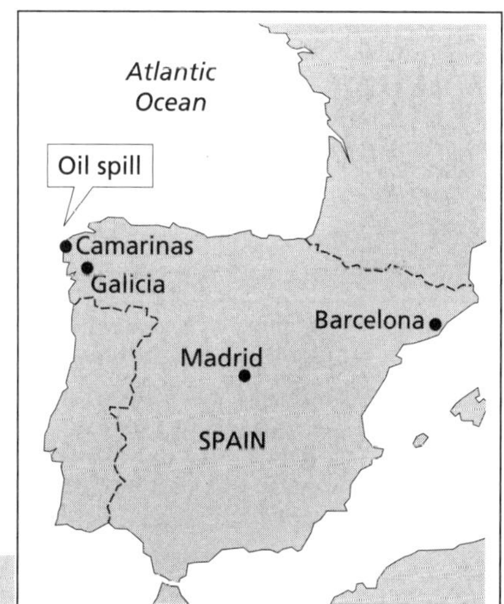

▶ *Map of Galician coast, Spain*

What are the consequences of acid rain, ozone depletion and global warming?

What are the effects of acid rain?

Acid rain damages buildings, plants, soils and waterways and people can inhale dry acid particles. Acid rain leaches out nutrients in the soils and dissolves heavy metals such as lead and mercury. Trees can be killed and acidified lakes and rivers may have little or no life left in them. Almost 80 per cent of lakes and rivers in Norway are acidified, probably due to pollution from the UK. Acid rain is spread by wind over a wide area away from the source of the pollution (e.g. from power stations).

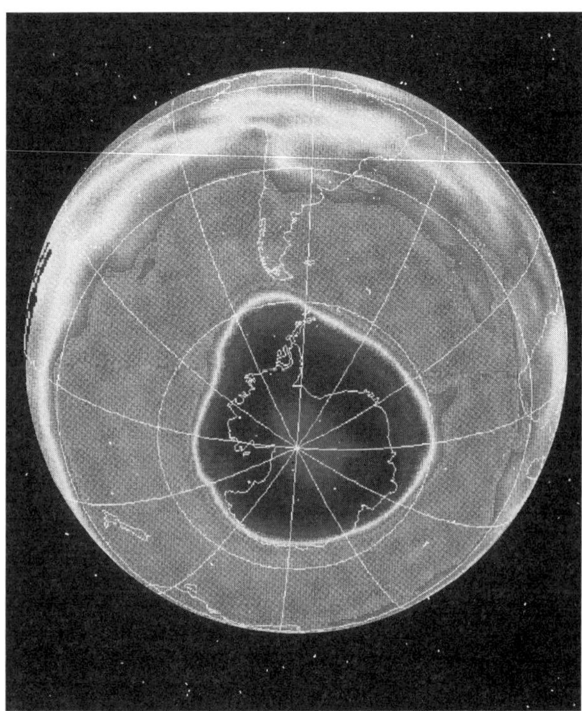

▲ *Ozone layer depletion*

How important is ozone depletion?

A thin ozone layer allows UV radiation from the sun to reach the Earth's surface and this can cause skin cancer and eye problems for people. Photosynthesis and plant growth are also reduced by increased radiation. The size of the ozone holes varies slightly each year and in 2002 they were slightly reduced. The global bans on the use of damaging chemicals (see page 103) will reduce the quantity of CFCs in the atmosphere but the pollutants last for 50 years and China and other LEDCs do not have to implement the restrictions until 2010.

How may global warming affect the way people live?

People have to adapt to climate changes and sea level rise but the problems will be different in MEDCs and LEDCs.

Agriculture	Basic crops such as wheat may be grown in new places but areas such as the Great Plains may grow less wheat as they become drier. Vines, maize and other crops traditionally grown in the Mediterranean may become widespread in the UK. Subsistence farmers in LEDCs will have fewer resources than MEDC farmers to be able to change the way they farm.
Tourism	People are attracted to hot, dry places for holidays and are less likely to travel to wet resorts, so changing climates will affect where people holiday and thus local income. Winter sports will have to change with warming and the resulting snow and glacier melt. Sea level rise could see the Maldive Islands disappear.
Increasing hazards, e.g. floods	Flooding of river valleys and coastal areas is becoming more frequent in many parts of the world (e.g. the UK and Europe each winter) as rainfall increases and more violent storms are experienced. The financial costs to people in MEDCs are high though the cost in lives is greater in LEDCs.
Sea level rise	Coastal erosion is affecting many parts of the UK coastline and houses and livelihoods are lost if coastal defence schemes are too expensive to build (e.g. Holderness Coast, East England). Most of Bangladesh is only a little above sea level and very poor so permanent defence schemes are not possible and people try to put in place local emergency plans. People in all parts of the world will have to change the way they live as sea level rises.

What are the effects of global warming on the natural environment?

Global warming is affecting the environment and so the way people live. Some of its effects include:

Climate change	In the 1990s Summer temperatures reached record levels around the globe. In 1998 on one day, Canada was 37°C, India 42°C, Japan 37°C and Saudi Arabia 46°C. In countries such as India people died from heat stroke.
Drought	Longer spells of dry weather and droughts are becoming more common in places such as India and East Africa with bad effects on subsistence farming.
Ice melt	In the Arctic and Antarctic ice melt is shrinking the icecaps and changing the circulation of the oceans. The North Atlantic Drift is changing its pattern of flow, which affects the climate of the UK. Glaciers are melting.
Storms and heavy rain	Storms are becoming more violent and more frequent around the globe, lasting longer and bringing more rain. Storms can result in storm surges hitting the coasts (e.g. Miami, USA) causing extensive damage and loss of life.
Sea level rise	A rise of 46 cm would put 92 million people at risk of flooding. Many European cities such as Venice would be threatened. The London Barrage is an attempt to stop London flooding when high tides, a storm surge and rising sea levels combine. The USA spends $30 million a year on coastal defence but gets $750 billion from coastal tourism. The global sea level is rising at about 2 mm/year and this seems to be accelerating with global warming. The UK average sea levels are expected to rise between 2 and 9 mm/year, possibly up to 67 cm by 2050.
Coral bleaching	Gradually warming seas cause reefs to die.
Changing plants and animals	The growing season for plants in the UK is longer, northern conifers die from heat, cottage gardens may only exist in northern England, birds nest in different places. Both natural and man-made landscapes are changing as overall temperatures rise.

Remember

You need to research one effect in detail. Use the Internet but be very selective in what you look for. For example, if you are researching global warming, search by using key words, such as *sea level rise UK*. Many international organizations, such as Greenpeace or Sierra Club, will have excellent details.

Case study

Coral reef bleaching

Coral reefs provide a habitat for 25 per cent of marine species and are one of the most productive ecosystems on Earth. Human threats from over-fishing and pollution contribute to the global decline of coral reefs but the biggest threat is from global and sea warming, which causes bleaching and eventually death. Reefs can recover but it can take years.

In 1998 the rise in sea temperature was 2°C in some places, which destroyed 15 per cent of world coral. The hottest sea temperatures ever recorded in the Great Barrier Reef, Australia resulted in widespread bleaching and up to 80 per cent death in some places. In 2002 AIMS (the Australian Institute of Marine Studies) gathered scientists together on Magnetic Island, Queensland, to improve and monitor the prediction of coral reef bleaching and to look at the links between climate change, sea temperatures, water currents and the biology of the Great Barrier Reef.

Most coral reefs are in poor countries that depend on tourism, for example Fiji's reefs where 65 per cent are bleached and 15 per cent dead. The threat to their environment and economy is great.

How can economic development be managed in a sustainable way?

What are sustainable strategies for development?

Sustainable strategies are those that enable development to take place to improve people's quality of life without permanent harm to the environment. Strategies will:

- try to manage existing harmful effects of development and prevent future problems through local, national and international agreements
- look for different ways of managing development in MEDCs and LEDCs, which may include alternative energy sources (e.g. wind farms, UK) to improving working conditions (e.g. Cubatao, Brazil).
- reduce resource consumption (recycling)

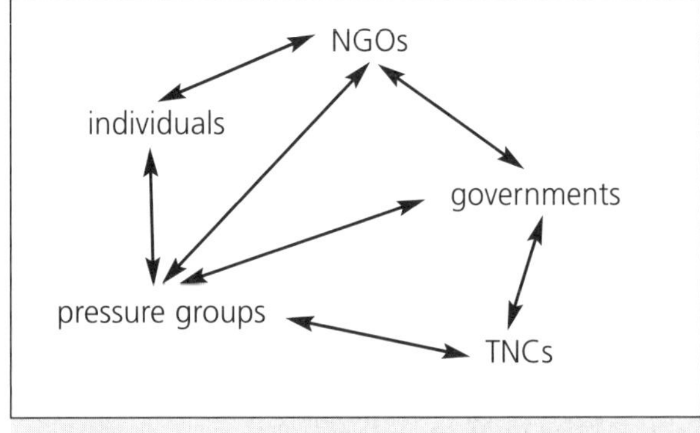

▲ *Who is involved?*

What sort of sustainable actions are being made in the UK?

- Reducing air pollution (e.g. through regulations to reduce emissions)
- Reducing water pollution in rivers and seas
- Increasing energy from renewable sources (e.g. target to increase the amount from wind)
- Increasing public transport to reduce number of cars and CO_2 discharge
- Reducing the use of cars (through, for example, increases in tax on petrol)
- Increasing number of energy efficient houses and buildings (e.g. houses in Milton Keynes, Tesco stores)
- Making changes in agriculture (e.g. reductions in nitrate use)
- Making greater use of alternative technology (e.g. solar powered buoys and wind farms, etc.).

Advantages of sustainable strategies for development

If every country followed sustainable strategies for development, the acceleration of major environmental global problems would be halted. International agreements can be effective. The increase in CFCs in the atmosphere has been slowed and the holes in the ozone layer became slightly smaller in 2002. Global conferences allow LEDCs as well as MEDCs to get together and discuss problems. LEDCs, affected by sea level rise, coral bleaching, increasing storms and flooding resulting from global warming (mostly caused by MEDC development) can put forward their views.

Different ways of managing development can be effective at local or national levels particularly in MEDCs, and have a global impact. Sustainable developments in LEDCs at local scales with appropriate technology can be cheap and efficient.

Disadvantages of sustainable strategies for development

International agreements are difficult to enforce. There is no global body that can make the USA agree to reduce vehicle emissions or reduce resource consumption. Many countries cannot afford to change to meet the agreements. MEDCs dominate global conferences and affect the agreements but most people in the world live in LEDCs. Coal is the main energy source in many LEDCs (e.g. India) and some MEDCs (e.g. Poland) and the cost of using alternatives to meet international agreement is too high.

People in MEDCs do not always like the changes that have to be made to follow sustainable strategies. To reduce petrol consumption and so vehicle emissions, the UK government increased the tax on petrol. This was very unpopular with people and increased the cost of travel and of transporting goods.

Can we be sustainable?

Sustainable strategies in MEDCs may require large-scale changes (e.g. alternative power generation, UK). LEDCs may see small-scale strategies being effective (e.g. village platforms, Mali).

Remember

You need to research one strategy in detail.

Definitions

Appropriate technology Technology appropriate to the needs, skills and knowledge of the people

Pressure groups Proactive groups which operate all the time, such as Friends of the Earth, Greepeace or reactive groups which gather together to oppose a particular harmful action such as a pollution leak (e.g. Sellafield)

Case study

MEDC

Neptune Network, Norway

On 20 November 2002 a millionaire hotel owner and member of Neptune Network, a green group, decided to take action in protest at the radioactive materials discharged into the sea from the nuclear plant at Sellafield, UK. He chained himself to part of a waste pipe from the outlet from Sellafield into the North Sea. Scandinavian countries have become increasingly alarmed that radioactive materials are being carried into their seas and fishing grounds. The Irish government have campaigned for many years for Sellafield to be closed and praised Greenpeace and other environmental groups for highlighting the dangers.

Can global conferences and international agreements have an effect?

Global conferences confirm the concern about the harmful effects of development and put forward changes. They are not always put into effect. Some countries will carry out the policies that have been agreed; others will not. The USA produces about a quarter of the world's pollution, but the government will not agree global controls already confirmed by Europe and other countries.

Conferences and agreements

1972 Stockholm UN Conference on the human environment raised awareness

1987 Montreal Protocol to phase out the use of ozone depleting chemicals is taking effect

1992 Copenhagen agreement committed governments to rapid end to using the most damaging CFCs in MEDCs, China 2010

1992 Earth Summit at Rio de Janeiros' global environmental discussions and set standards that led to Agenda 21 being included local authority development plans

1997 Kyoto Conference continued to consider climate change controls though USA did not ratify

2000, **2001** global conferences to try to get ratification of previous agreements to reduce emissions

2002 Earth Summit Johannesburg discussed environmental problems, though NGOs pessimistic about outcomes

Case study

LEDC

Gas buses in Delhi, India

A quarter of Delhi people have breathing problems from air pollution, so in April 2001 a September deadline was set for all buses to convert to CNG, compressed natural gas, a cleaner fuel. 12 000 public transport buses were needed and 55 000 auto-rickshaws. The deadline was not met, however. There were too few gas stations or converted buses and thousands of people could not get to work. There were riots, buses were burnt and those that did run were dangerously crowded.

Delhi choking on CNG order

Patience is running out in Delhi, following a shortage of buses after a Supreme Court order permitting only CNG vehicles on the capital's roads.

Mobs torched six buses belonging to the Delhi Transport Corporation and broke window panes of several buses in West Delhi. Tuesday morning saw office-goers and students waiting in desperation for the few buses available out of the 12 000 strong fleet Delhi has. Similarly, only a fraction of the 55 000 auto-rickshaws was on the roads.

Delhi's buses have been cruel to schoolchildren, killing many in a spate of accidents. And today, after waiting for a bus for hours, the children at a grave risk to their safety had to compete with a maddening crowd of adults to find a place in jam-packed buses or hang on footboards.

▲ *Newslink on Internet*

Making the grade

Getting down to revision

Before you start, you must know the following:

- the Geography GCSE specification
- the difference between the two examination papers
- the structure of the examination papers.

Check your material

Go through your books and check that you have underlined headings and side headings and that any bullet points are numbered. You could highlight main headings to separate sections. Writing, without headings, is more difficult to learn. Maps and diagrams without headings/annotation may not mean very much to you. Check that you have sufficient work on each section to revise. If not, ask someone who has or use textbooks or the internet to build up your resources. You cannot write on the examination paper 'I was away for this bit'!

You should plan to begin your revision weeks before the examinations but most people find themselves with too little time, too late, to fit in all they want to do. Whenever you begin to revise, draw up a calendar of the days/weeks to the exam and plan to revise a little each day.

How do people learn?

People all learn things in different ways:

- Some people may be able to read through the information slowly, and remember it. Most people cannot.
- Some people can remember detail for a long time but most people need to reinforce learning by going back over work frequently.
- Multi-sensory learning is effective, using sight (diagrams, maps, photographs), sound (talking to each other) and feeling (count bullet points on your fingers).
- Try making very brief notes on cards, use subheadings and learn those, so that in an exam the memory of these revision notes may help you recall a lot more detail.
- Try drawing a mind map that will help you sort the information in your mind into useable chunks.
- Read your work out loud or discuss it with a friend. Argue an issue through, what would happen if…?
- Work with a friend and test each other. Work out a question to ask, say it and think about the answer. This will help to reinforce your own learning (assuming you both know the right answer!).
- Facts in groups of 3, 5 or 7 are generally easier to learn than in 4, 6 or 8. Revise 5 facts about something counting with your fingers to reinforce the learning.

Do make the effort to revise. In an examination you cannot hope to remember everything, but recall of some detail and the context in which it can be used will give you confidence to keep writing.

Do not rely on your memory of the past two years or think that reading through the work the night before will be sufficient!

Exam practice questions

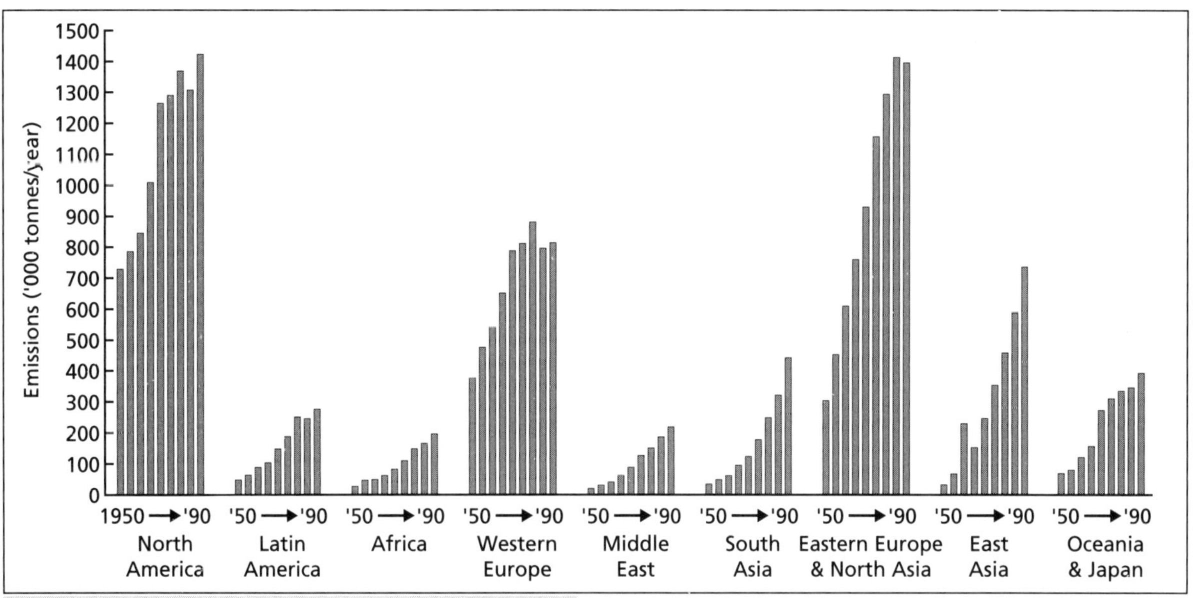

▲ *Figure 1 Carbon emissions from 1950–2000*

1 Study Figure 1 and use it to answer 1(a) and (b):

a) Name the area contributing the least carbon emissions in 2000. (1 mark)

b) Name the area which has contributed the most carbon emissions since 1950. (1 mark)

c) Suggest ways in which carbon emissions contribute to global environmental damage. (6 marks)

d) Suggest ways in which carbon emissions can be reduced. (6 marks)

2 One consequence of global warming is sea level rise. Describe how people can be affected by sea level rise. (6 marks)

3 Sustainable strategies are needed in managing sustainable global economic development. Describe and explain one such strategy for managing economic development. (6 marks)

4 Suggest ways in which environmental pressure groups may influence governments. (4 marks)

12 Tourism and the economy

Why has there been a growth of holiday destinations?

The development of tourist destinations

1960s
Rapid growth of Mediterranean coastal holidays, including southern Spain, France, Italy and Greece. These areas were able to offer totally organized, cheap holidays with the guarantee of hot, dry weather.

1970s
Development of existing European resorts and further development in places like Portugal and Turkey. The North African coastal areas of Tunisia and Morocco became increasingly popular. Long-haul holidays grew with the USA the most popular destination.

1980s
The tourism industry expanded throughout the whole of the Mediterranean region and increasing numbers of people visiting the USA. Less economically developed parts of the world, such as the Caribbean Islands and Goa (India), became increasingly popular.

1990s
Increasing development of tourism throughout the developed world and in many parts of the developing world. Growth of interest in different cultural and physical areas, such as China and Alaska.

Key facts

What is a package holiday?

A holiday where everything is organized by a travel agent, including travel, accommodation, car(s) and any other services. One price is paid for the complete package.

- Tourism is one of the fastest growing global industries.
- Tourism creates many jobs, both directly and indirectly.
- Over-development can damage coastal areas and discourage visitors.

Why has there been a growth in global tourism?

- Air transport destinations have developed throughout the world with more regional airports.
- Airfares have become cheaper.
- People have more money to spend on holidays.
- People have longer holidays and can travel to distant places or visit a number of places on one holiday.
- The growth of package tours to all parts of the world has made organizing holidays much easier.
- Specialist travel agents can arrange holidays to more remote places.
- There is an increased awareness of a wider range of places because of holiday programmes on television and travel reports in newspapers.
- Many parts of the world have developed holiday destinations or special attractions because they recognize that tourism is important to the local economy.

How important are physical factors to holiday destinations?

Although there has been a growth in holidays linked to cities, theme parks and sport, physical factors such as climate and scenery still play a major part in holiday destinations.

Climate is particularly important if people want beach holidays or winter sport holidays. Look at the following climate data for Malaga, in Southern Spain:

Malaga, Spain	J	F	M	A	M	J	J	A	S	O	N	D
Mean temp (°C)	10	12	15	17	20	25	28	28	25	20	15	12
Sunshine hours	6	7	6	8	9	11	12	11	8	7	6	5
Rainfall (mm)	60	58	54	56	41	8	0	4	18	59	66	81

What are the advantages of Malaga as a holiday destination?

- Summers are hot and winters mild.
- Rainfall is very low during the summer months.
- The area has high sunshine amounts for six months of the year.

Scenery can make an area attractive or spectacular and is particularly important for beach or sightseeing holidays. The following photograph illustrates the importance of scenery to holiday destinations.

How important is tourism to LEDCs?

- Tourism brings in much needed money.
- The development of tourism can generate jobs in the building industry.
- Many people are employed as a result of tourism either directly (in hotels/theme parks) or indirectly (local shops/services/agriculture/making souvenirs).
- The development of tourism can improve local infrastructure (roads/railways/airports).
- Money brought in by tourism can be used to improve social facilities such as schools and health centres.

What are the consequences of tourism development?

Case study

MEDC

The impacts of tourism in Spain

Why did the tourism industry develop in Southern Spain?

The number of visitors to Spain has increased by over 40 million people a year since 1950.

The major reasons for this are:

- the attractive climate (hot, dry summers)
- hundreds of miles of beach with warm sea temperatures
- easy access from other European countries
- the relatively low price of holidays
- spectacular inland scenery and coastal nightlife.

▶ *Costa del Sol*

Costa del Sol

'The coast of the sun' is aptly named, since it enjoys probably the best year-round weather in Europe. This coastline has been extensively developed but offers superb holiday amenities and accommodation to suit every taste and pocket.'

◀ *From a holiday brochure*

What were the impacts of the growth of tourism?

In the 1960s the Spanish government realized that tourism could bring significant economic benefit to southern Spain and encouraged its development.

Positive impacts

- The creation of many jobs in hotels/restaurants
- A boost to industries linked to tourism (building/transport/shops/agriculture)
- The development of new industries supplying the tourism industry
- The development of new infrastructure (roads/railways/airports)
- A general increase in living standards.

Negative impacts

- Destruction of the environment for building hotels/resorts
- Overdevelopment in some areas
- Pollution on beaches and in the Mediterranean Sea
- Over-use of resources, especially water which led to rationing for local people and agriculture
- Jobs are often seasonal and insecure.

Recent developments

The tourism crisis

By the late 1980s – 1990s it was clear that Spain's popularity as a holiday destination was beginning to decline:

- Many resorts were overcrowded with poor accomodation.
- Beaches were dirty and, in some areas, raw sewage discharged into the sea was causing health problems.
- Other Mediterranean areas, such as Turkey or Greece, provided better-quality and cheaper beach holidays.

The regeneration of tourism

'A Plan for Spanish Tourism' was implemented by the Ministry of Industry to regenerate the industry. Measures included:

- a ban on the building of any new hotels, unless they are 4 or 5 star quality
- stricter building regulations that stop the building of high-rise hotels and ensure more open space between buildings
- the upgrading of water supplies and sewage disposal
- an improvement in sea-water quality and beach cleanliness

Case study

LEDC

The impacts of tourism in south-east Africa

Wildlife tourism (Kenya and Tanzania)
Kenya and Tanzania have protected a great deal of their land by designating it as National Parks and Game Reserves. These attract many visitors to the area on safari holidays.

Advantages to the area:
- provides a major source of income and many jobs
- provides a market for local goods
- helps to protect wild animals
- money is used to provide local schools and healthcare.

Disadvantages to the area:
- The environment can be damaged by over-use
- Animals can be disturbed and forced to move away
- Nomadic tribes have been forced off their land
- Local people can be exploited.

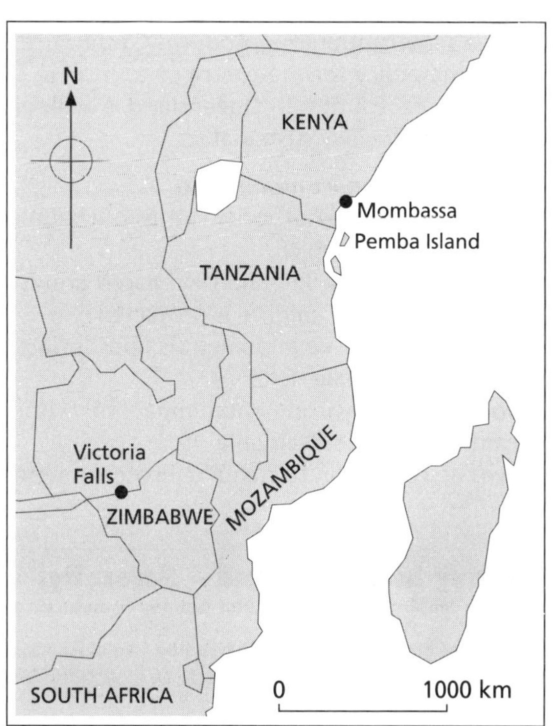

▲ *Map of East Africa*

Beach holidays – Mombasa (Kenya)
The area around Mombasa is especially popular for beach holidays, with many people coming to explore the coral reefs and marine life. The growth of tourism has given a massive boost to the local economy, providing work for nearly 20 per cent of the population. It has helped to develop the local building and transport industries. However, this growth has many disadvantages, including:
- increase in road development and traffic
- loss of farmland, natural vegetation and wildlife habitats for new buildings
- damage of the fragile coral reef by divers, and pollution from boats
- loss of farmland has led to the movement of traditional farmers
- break-up of families as young men move to the coast to work in the tourism industry.

Ecoheaven – Pemba Island
Pemba Island is known as 'Emerald Isle'. A new resort has been built in a nature reserve where visitors can explore mangrove swamps and forest and see bush babies, eagles and parrots. The reserve also has a 5 km strip of white sandy beach and offers the opportunity for diving and sea fishing. The resort has only 20 chalets built in the forest to fit in with the natural environment and designed to cause as little damage as possible.

How can tourism be managed sustainably?

Case study

MEDC

Ecotourism in Queensland, Australia

The Queensland Ecotourism Plan 2003–2008: Sustainable tourism in Queensland's natural areas was launched on 22 October 2002 at Australia's International Ecotourism Conference in Cairns. This plan outlines the policy for the future of tourism in Queensland. Its purpose is to ensure ecotourism in Queensland is ecologically, commercially, culturally and socially sustainable.

Environmental impact monitoring

Queensland Tourism Authority carries out regular Environmental Impact Monitoring which:

- monitors both marine and land based areas to ensure that the environment and wildlife is protected
- ensures that any development is appropriate to the local area in both size and scale
- monitors the environmental impact of visitors to ensure that Queensland's ecotourism industry continues to be sustainable
- gives accreditation to genuine ecotourism and nature-based tourism operators.

Definitions

Conservation The protection and improvement of natural and human landscapes

Ecotourism Tourism that does not damage the local environment or cultures

Sustainability Development that allows people and environments long-term survival

Holiday in Queensland – Naturally!

If you're looking for a spectacular holiday in nature's theme park, you can't go past Queensland!

Where else but Queensland will you find five of Australia's 14 World Heritage Areas – protected because of their unique environmental values, and known worldwide because of their awe-inspiring beauty:

- **Fraser Island** – the world's largest sand island featuring white beaches flanked by strikingly coloured sand cliffs, tall rainforests and freshwater lakes.
- **The Wet Tropics** – a 900 000 hectare living rainforest museum showcasing the ecological and evolutionary processes that shaped Australian plant and animal life.
- **The Great Barrier Reef** – the world's largest World Heritage Area is made up of some 2800 individual reefs and is home to an estimated 1500 species of fish, more than 700 species of hard, reef-building corals and sponges and over 4000 mollusc species, as well as whales, turtles and dolphins.
- **Riversleigh Fossil Fields** – one of the world's richest fossil mammal records.
- **Central Eastern Rainforest Reserves of Australia** – almost 60 000 hectares of ancient rainforest on the Border Ranges featuring prehistoric ferns, conifers and flowering plants, this region is home to endangered frogs and primitive bird species.

Kingfisher Bay Resort Fraser Island Queensland

Australia's World Heritage listed Fraser Island – the world's largest sand island – is no desert!

1 Magnificent rainforest
2 Beautiful fresh water lakes
3 Mighty sand dunes
4 Spectacular Seventy-Five Mile Beach
5 Shipwrecks and abundant wildlife
6 Surf and calm, blue island waters
7 Paradise for boating, fishing, swimming, beachcombing and bushwalking.

Ranger-guided eco-tours

Expert informative rangers guide full and half-day ecotours

1 Swim in clear, freshwater lakes
2 Walk through towering rain forests
3 Wander around fast flowing creeks
4 See mighty sandblows and magnificent coloured sands
5 Discover some of the 325 recorded bird species
6 Learn about the Aboriginal and European history of the island
7 Taste bush food

Extracts from Kingfisher Bay Resort and Village. Visit www.heinemann.co.uk/hotlinks for more information.

Case study

CAMPFIRE – Zimbabwe

LEDC

Zimbabwe relies on visitors from overseas, a quarter of whom come from the UK and Ireland. In 1999, two million tourists came to visit the country's mountains, forests and game reserves, and the tourist industry employed around 200 000 people.

Almost 5 million people live in semi-arid lands covering almost half of Zimbabwe. Despite the dryness and difficult conditions, a wide range of wildlife is found here. CAMPFIRE (Communal Areas Management Programme for Indigenous Resources) is a programme designed to assist rural development and conservation.

The CAMPFIRE movement began in the mid 1980s. It encourages local communities to make their own decisions about wildlife management and control. It aims to help people manage natural resources so that plants, animals and people – the whole ecosystem – all benefit.

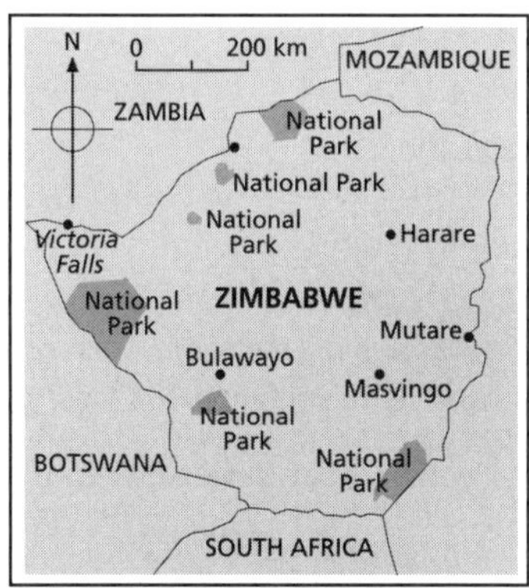

▲ *Map of Zimbabwe*

Success through CAMPFIRE

Tourism development has helped many of Zimbabwe's poorer rural communities. Through CAMPFIRE, foreign visitors buy licences to hunt wildlife within certain quotas. As well as keeping wildlife numbers at sustainable limits, the profits from these licences and the sale of meat and skins of the animals is ploughed back into local communities to build new schools, wells and health clinics.

Trophy hunting is considered to be the ultimate form of ecotourism, as hunters usually travel in small groups, demand few amenities, cause minimal damage to the local ecosystem, yet provide considerable income

CAMPFIRE operates on land inhabited by 250 000 people across 22 districts. But as wildlife populations can only tolerate a certain amount of sport-hunting, CAMPFIRE is diversifying into other forms of tourism to help rural communities. For example, Sunungukai camp near Harare offers visitors the chance to stay in traditional round huts, share meals with local residents, go on hikes with local guides, and spot wildlife.

Extract from www.globaleye.org.uk published by Worldaware

Case study

Ecotourism – Ecuador

Visit www.heinemann.co.uk/hotlinks for more information.

LEDC

RAINFOREST CONCERN

Conserving and protecting threatened natural habitats

Ecotourism project in Santa Lucia – Ecuadorian rainforest

With the help of international and local conservation organizations, Santa Lucia has undertaken its first sustainable development project – an ecotourism operation. The natural beauty of Santa Lucia's cloud forest made ecotourism a logical choice to provide a sustainable source of income for the community. This income will enable the community to continue to conserve the cloud forest under their care, while at the same time sharing its treasures with others.

Funds for the purchase of key parcels of land were provided by Rainforest Concern, a British conservation organization. With their help, Santa Lucia has been able to construct an Ecolodge with facilities for up to 20 visitors. The Ecolodge was built in the traditional local style, using sustainably harvested wood. It provides comfortable accommodation, hot water showers and a wide porch with hammocks.

The lodge is lit by candlelight at night, though in the future Santa Lucia hopes to install a sustainable electrical system based on renewable energy.

The Ecolodge can be reached only on foot, via a hike of approximately 2 hours from the nearest village. Backpacks and other heavy bags are brought up by mulepack, so that visitors can enjoy the views and birding opportunities along the way.

▲ *Location of Ecuador*

Extract from Rainforestconcern

Making the grade

Developing your answers

Higher mark questions are usually marked using levels of marking which means the more developed your answer the higher the level you will achieve. It is important to appreciate what is required to reach the next level.

The levels are usually described as:

LEVEL 1 – BASIC	LEVEL 2 – CLEAR	LEVEL 3 – DETAILED
• Limited knowledge • Simple understanding of the question • Limited development of ideas	• Some accurate knowledge • Clear understanding of the question • Shows some development of ideas	• Accurate, well located knowledge • Thorough understanding of the question • Developed ideas linked to the question

Example question

Using LEDC examples you have studied explain the disadvantages of tourism. (6 marks)

Level 1 Response (1–2 marks)

'Tourism can bring many disadvantages including problems of litter and overcrowding. Tourists often don't look after places very well and can create problems for local people.'

This answer does not use examples and could be about anywhere! It makes a small number of undeveloped points. (1 mark)

Level 2 Response (3–4 marks)

'The growth of tourism in Goa (India) has created many jobs and brought a lot of money to the area. However, new building has spoilt the environment and there has been an increase in pollution, especially litter and sewage, which goes into the sea. Lots of the jobs created are seasonal.'

This answer mentions one place which is appropriate. The jobs and money part are advantages so are not relevant. It has some environmental points which are slightly developed and brings in the problem of seasonal jobs. (3 marks)

Level 3 Response (5–6 marks)

'The development of tourism in areas like Goa (Western India) and Kenya (East Africa) has brought many disadvantages. In Goa the continued building of hotels has spoilt the environment and brought increased problems of pollution with sewage being pumped into the sea. Jobs have been created, but these are often low paid and seasonal. Also there is often conflict with local people who have their water rationed and are often stopped from using the beach. In Kenya the growth of safari holidays has put pressure on the wild animals and damaged the vegetation. Also local tribes have been moved from their land. On the coast increasing numbers of visitors are damaging the fragile coral.'

This answer uses two well located examples and appreciates that there are both safari and beach holidays in Kenya. There are a number of well-developed points which are appropriate to the question. (6 marks)

Exam practice questions

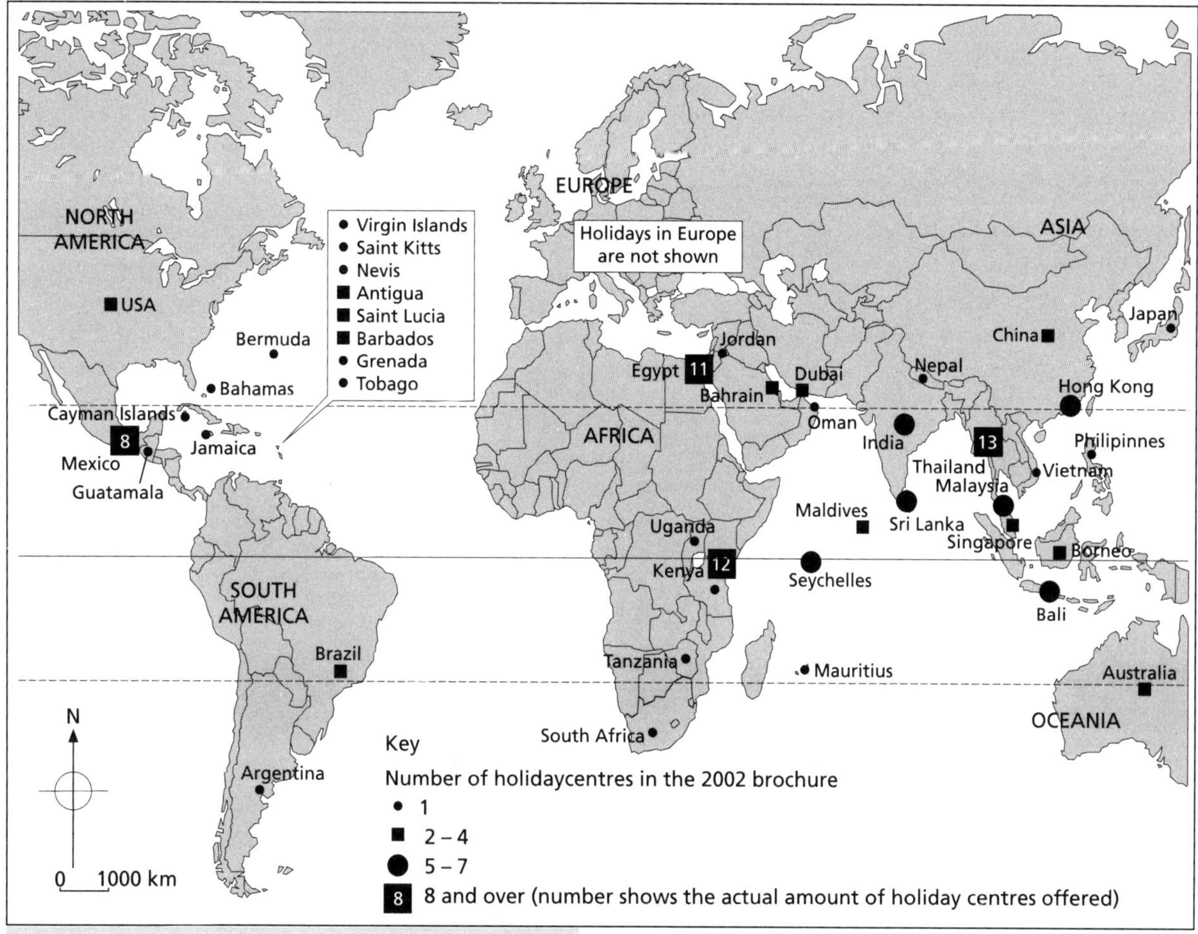

▲ *Figure 1 World map showing holiday centres*

1 Study Figure 1, which shows the number of holiday centres in different countries in a 2002 holiday brochure featuring LEDCs and use it to answer questions 1(a) and (b).

a) In which country are the most holiday centres offered? (1 mark)

b) Describe the pattern of holiday destinations shown on the map. (4 marks)

c) Suggest why there has been a growth in holidays in LEDCs in recent years. (4 marks)

2 **a)** What is meant by 'Ecotourism'? (2 marks)

b) Describe one example of ecotourism that you have studied. (4 marks)

3 Explain how physical features might encourage the development of tourism in an area. (6 marks)

4 Using examples you have studied describe the advantages and disadvantages that tourism has brought to local economies. (6 marks)

5 Using an example you have studied:

a) Explain how tourism can put pressure on the environment. (4 marks)

b) Explain how the environmental effects of tourism can be managed. (6 marks)

Revise your map reading

An Ordnance Survey (OS) map extract may be used in either of the final examinations. If it is used it will be at 1:50 000 scale and include a key.

Examiners can use Ordnance Survey maps for questions that test:

1 map reading skills
2 the ability to use or interpret a map.

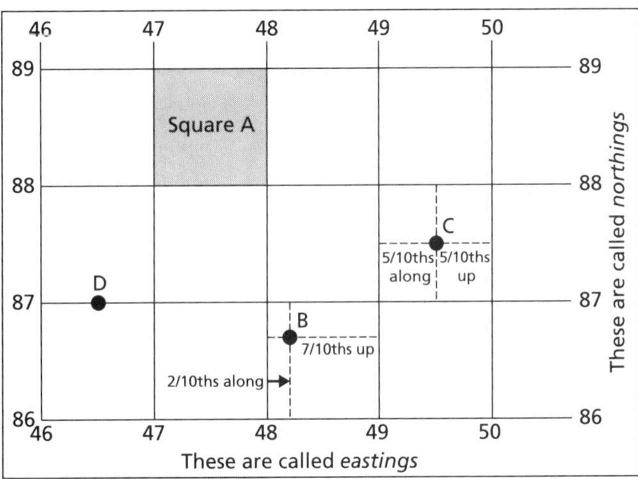

▲ *Figure 1*

1 Map reading skills

To make the best use of an OS map, a number of skills are required. These include the ability to:

- read conventional signs
- use grid references
- use scale and calculate distance
- use compass directions
- interpret relief (shape of the land).

Reading conventional signs

Conventional signs are symbols and colours showing features on a map.

Using grid references

Every OS map is covered by grid lines. These enable particular points on the map to be located.

How to use grid references:

- Always start from the bottom left-hand corner of the square
- Always quote eastings before northings. ('Along the corridor and up the stairs!')

Four-figure references describe a whole square, so in Figure 1 the reference for square A is 4788.

Six-figure references describe a point and are read by subdividing a square into 10 further eastings and northings, each representing 100 m. The method is the same: the third and sixth numbers are the tenths. So, in Figure 1 the reference for point B is 482867, and for point C is 495875. If the point lies on a grid line, a zero must be used – so the reference for point D is 465870.

Using scale and calculating distance

Scale is the relationship between distance on the map and distance on the ground. By measuring the distance between two points and using the scale-line at the bottom of the map, the real distance can be calculated. *Always remember* to state the unit being measured (kilometres).

Key fact

Whatever the scale of an OS map one grid square always represents 1km^2

Using compass directions

All OS maps have north at the top. As a minimum the eight compass directions (Figure 2) should be known. In order to find the direction between two places, put the centre of the compass on the starting place and read off the direction to the finishing place.

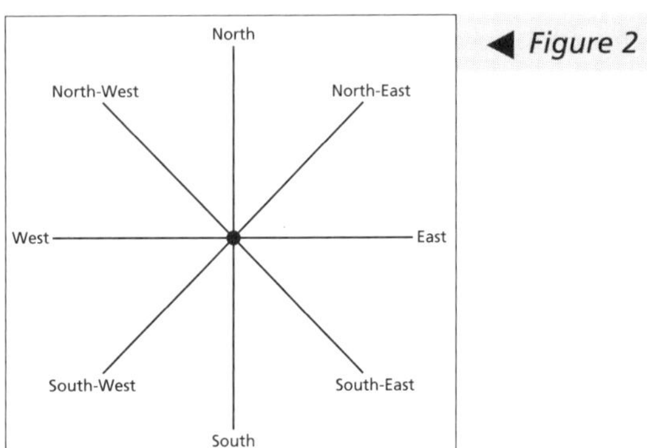

◀ *Figure 2*

Remember

Use your map skills (e.g. when describing a settlement, use grid references to locate it, scale to say how big it is and direction to give the position of nearby places).

Interpreting relief (shape of the land)

Height is shown on a map by:

- spot heights
- triangulation pillars
- contour lines.

Key points about contour lines

- On a 1:50 000 OS map contour lines are 10 m apart
- Contour lines cannot cross
- Every fifth contour line is thicker
- The numbers on contour lines face upslope
- Contour lines close together = steep slope
- Contour lines further apart = more gentle slope.

2 Map interpretation

Interpretation is the way a map is used to describe or explain something. The type of interpretation required will often be determined by the map extract.

For example:

- A map that has rivers and coasts on it may be used to ask questions about physical geography or tourism.
- A map that has a rural landscape on it may be used to ask questions about settlements (villages) or communication networks.
- A map of an industrial area may be used to ask questions about types and locations of industry.
- A map of an urban area may be used to ask questions about land use change and urban growth.

Practise your map-reading skills

1 Name the farm found in grid square 8875. (1 mark)

2 Give the four figure grid reference for the square containing Warkton village. (1 mark)

3 Name the features at:
a) 857795 **b)** 893798 (2 marks)

4 Which direction are the following places from Kettering Railway Station (864780)
a) Leisure Village (858774)
b) Wicksteed Park (8876) (2 marks)

5 What is the straight-line distance, to the nearest km, from Kettering Station to:
a) Pytchley Lodge (876753)
b) Weekley Village (8880). (2 marks)

6 Name two ways that height is shown on the map. (2 marks)

7 Describe the physical geography in grid square 8576. (4 marks)

8 Describe the human geography in grid square 8579. (4 marks)

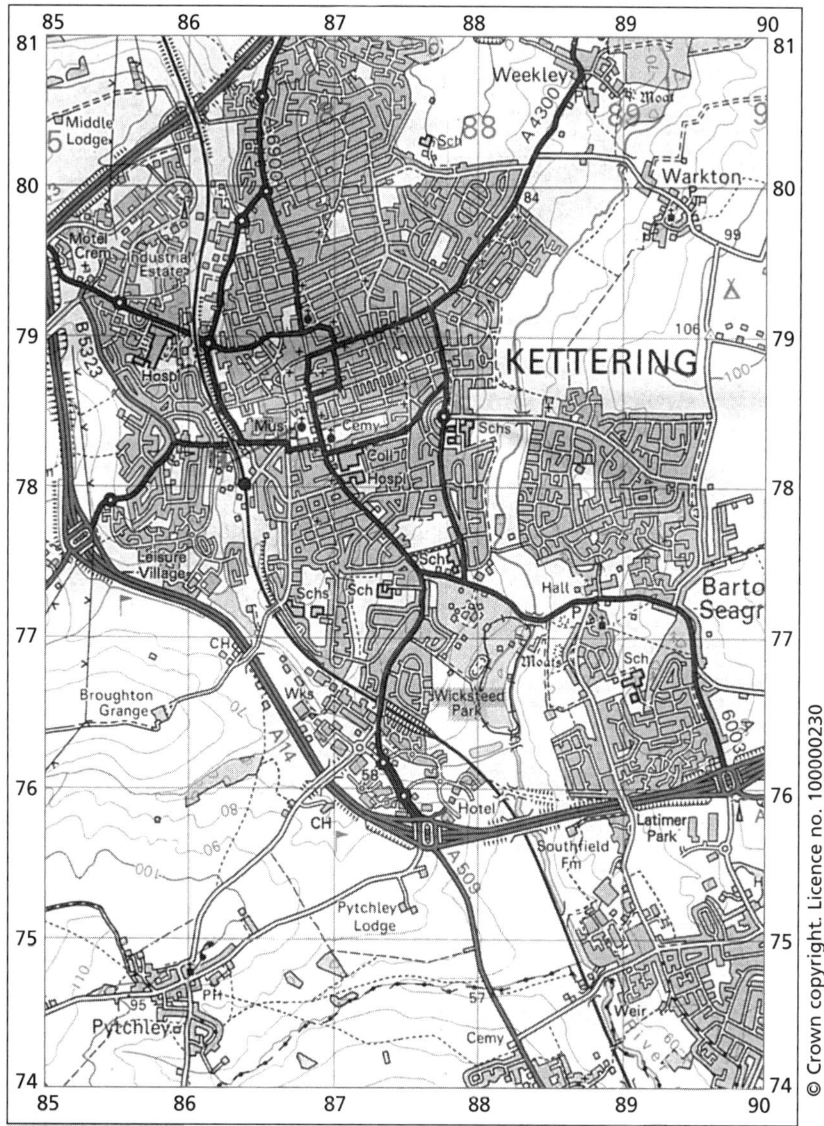

▲ *Figure 3*

Scale 1:50 000

Mark schemes

Exam practice – Decision-making exercise (pages 8–11)

1 **a)** Two marks for each of OIL: COAL: GAS
One mark for the general trend – oil and gas increased; coal decreased.
Second mark for changes to trend; rate of change and use of data (3 x 2) (6 marks)

b) Bar chart: all bars (7) accurate and fully labelled = 4 marks
5/6 bars accurate and fully labelled = 3 marks
3/4 bars accurate and fully labelled = 2 marks
1/2 bars accurate and fully labelled = 1 mark
A maximum of 2 marks when the graph is not labelled (4 marks)

c) Focus is electricity – not cars (oil)

Level 1 (1–2). General points about having more appliances with some examples (televisions/computers/kitchen appliances).

Level 2 (3–4). General points about appliances and broader ideas about increases in wealth/more housing/more recreational facilities, etc. (4 marks)

2 **a)** Idea of using them again – 1 mark
Idea of not running out – 1 mark (2 marks)

b) Points mark – max 2 for any type (solar/wind/micro)
Max 1 in any type if no advantages or disadvantages

Possible answers	**Advantages**	**Disadvantages**
Solar	clean/non polluting	expensive/subject to weather
Wind	suitable areas/non-polluting	small amounts/noisy/unattractive
Micro	clean/non-polluting/cheap	damage to environment

3 **a)** **(i)** 3154 (1 mark)
(ii) 306587/308555 (2 marks)
(iii) Golf course
Place of worship with a tower (2 marks)
(iv) Contour lines
Spot Heights
Triangular pillar (2 x 1) (2 marks)
(v) North-East (N.E.) (1 mark)
(vi) 3 km (1 mark)

b) Points mark (4 x 1)
Any points could include:

- Camping sites
- Caravan sites
- Tropical Bird Garden
- Marina
- Museum
- Ferry (summer only)
- Holiday camp
- Beach

(4 marks)

c) *Level 1 (1–2).* Lowland area, rivers, marsh
Level 2 (3–4). Low-lying with slight hill in north
River and small streams/marsh
Tidal estuary (4 marks)

d) *Level 1 (1–2).* Limited understanding of the idea: environmentally sensitive. Tends to describe the area in terms of open countryside.

Level 2 (3–4). Clear appreciation of a lowland area of wetland, which could be farmland and also open land for wildlife, especially birds. Flat land means that it is sensitive to damaged views. (4 marks)

4 a) *Level 1 (1–2).* Basic idea about creating jobs in the area through building and management.

Level 2 (3–4). Develops the idea to include some understanding of the multipliers and brings in linked job boost for the area (local industry, local shops and services, etc) (4 marks)

b) *Level 1 (1–2).* Basic idea about why some people may not like it with clear reference to the resources. Limited understanding of conflict.

Level 2 (3–4). Clear appreciation of local conflict and uses resources to explain why people might have a difference of opinion. 'people looking for jobs might be pleased about the development but owners of a holiday business might not because it could damage their business.' (4 marks)

5 *Level 1 (1–3).* Basic repeat of data, which shows limited development and does not consider the range of factors. Tends to focus on one/two resources.

Level 2 (4–6). Good use of a range of resources with clear quotes carefully selected to make a case. A well constructed view that considers both economic and environmental impacts, although not always balanced. Some original ideas beyond the resources.

Level 3 (6–9). Excellent use of resources to support decision. Detailed quotes to illustrate both economic and environmental impacts. Considers both advantages and disadvantages to come to a balanced decision. Original ideas that go beyond the resources. (9 marks)

Chapter 1 – Population change (pages 14–21)

1 a) Natural increase Egypt 21, France 3 (2 marks)

b) Lower, Bangladesh, Brazil (3 marks)

2 a) Migration is movement of people from one place to another, often permanently (1 mark)

b) *Level 1 (1–2).* Basic ideas linking death rates, healthcare, long life expectancy, MEDC, reduction of infant mortality LEDC

Level 2 (3–4). Clear explanation, relevant data, some exemplification, ageing population MEDC, LEDC young population growing, few old people, low death rate (4 marks)

c) *Level 1 (1–2).* Basic ideas, birth rates high LEDCs, example, simple data, MEDC, low birth rate, small families, limited example

Level 2 (3–4). Explanation of factors affecting birth rates, differences, MEDC and LEDC, development, some examples (4 marks)

d) *Level 1 (1–2).* Basic ideas of push/pull concept and push ideas, e.g. natural hazards, famine, farming changes, attraction of better life style, limited examples

Level 2 (3–4). Clear explanation, problems rural areas, understanding links, physical and human factors, and push factors. Clear understanding of attractions of urban areas, improved quality of life, examples (4 marks)

e) *Level 1 (1–2).* Simplistic, basic statements of problems in LEDCs with high population growth, and problems caused by lack of housing, clean water, employment etc, pressure on land.

Level 2 (3–4). Showing a clear understanding, including a description of LEDC city problems and congestion, pollution with reference to shanty towns, pressure on services, health care and education.

Level 3 (5–6). Providing a detailed description with some explanation of relevant material problems in LEDCs, the links between problems and some indications of causes, including the growth of shanty towns, poverty in rural areas. (6 marks)

f) *Level 1 (1–2)*. Simple, basic ideas (must refer to MEDC) some reference to management and government actions.

Level 2 (3–4). Clear understanding of problems of ageing population, healthcare, housing, reference to managing change, some examples

Level 3 (5–6). Detailed understanding, relevant material, reasons, links in population change between birth rate, death rate and life expectancy, life expectancy, aging population, increase dependency, changing service provision, examples, detailed, relevant. (6 marks)

Chapter 2 – Rural–urban migration (pages 22–29)

1 a) Better education, more houses, better health care, communications and power, more wealth, (any two of these) (2 marks)

b) The movement of people from rural areas to an urban areas, because of factors, (see push/pull) (2 marks)

2 a) *Level 1 (1–2)*. Basic statements, 2 reasons for leaving rural area, e.g. poverty, natural hazards, limited description

Level 2 (3–4). Describes 2 factors (4 marks)

b) *Level 1 (1–2)*. Basic, two problems stated, e.g. loss of working age group, dependant people left in rural areas, lack of skilled workers, depopulation

Level 2 (3–4). Clearly describes two problems (4 marks)

3 *Level 1 (1–2)*. Basic, simple ideas about rapid growth of cities, statement of problems, e.g. congestion, overcrowding, lack of services, lack of clean water.

Level 2 (3–4). Description of range of problems in shanty towns and urban areas with reference to a specific example.

Level 3 (5–6). Detailed description of range of problems, plus the use of references to examples (6 marks)

4 *Level 1 (1–2)*. Basic understanding of shanty towns, simple statement of problems e.g. poor housing, lack of clean water, no sewage systems, overcrowding, limited exemplification.

Level 2 (3–4). Clear appreciation of problems for people living in shanty towns, with examples.

Level 3 (5–6). Detailed description of problems and clear understanding of shanty towns, of problems of living, well located examples. (6 marks)

5 *Level 1 (1–2)*. Basic ideas stating how life might be improved shanty towns e.g., clean water, new houses, limited examples.

Level 2 (3–4). Clear appreciation of ways in which quality of life may be improved through a variety of schemes, reference to examples.

Level 3 (5–6). Describes a number of ways in which a shanty town may be improved with detailed understanding of links between self help/government/NGO schemes, examples used. (6 marks)

Chapter 3 – Changing town and city centres (pages 30–37)

1 a) Named, located (1 mark)

b) Statement of reason (1 mark)

c) *Level 1 (1–2)*. Basic ideas about inner city areas and problems of living in tower blocks, reference to three problems.

Level 2 (3–4). Clear understanding of three problems, reference to inner city, and tower blocks, reference to Hulme, Manchester.

Level 3 (5–6). Detailed description of three problems, clear understanding of problems of living in inner city area or in tower blocks, reference to Hulme. (6 marks)

2 *Level 1 (1–2).* Basic statement of ideas of inner city and problems e.g., housing, transport, decay, limited reference to examples.

Level 2 (3–4). Develops ideas to describe problems, demonstrates understanding of decline in inner city, reference to examples.

Level 3 (5–6). Clear description of problems, with detailed appreciation of inner city and reasons for decline, well located examples. (6 marks)

3 *Level 1 (1–2).* Basic statement of ideas about pedestrianization and public transport in MEDC cities, limited reference to management or change.

Level 2 (3–4). Clear consideration of ways managing city centres using pedestrianization and public transport, understanding of change and issues of management.

Level 3 (5–6). Detailed appreciation of management of change in MEDC city centre and links between pedestrianization, public transport and traffic. (6 marks)

4 *Level 1 (1–2).* Simplistic statement about scheme, limited reference to meeting peoples needs, named, not well-located place.

Level 2 (3–4). Develops ideas, some detail, reference to people's needs and consideration of scheme in meeting needs, scheme identified.

Level 3 (5–6). Detailed description of scheme, excellent understanding of how scheme might meet people's needs, well-located, identified scheme. (6 marks)

Chapter 4 – Pressure at the rural–urban fringe (pages 38–45)

1 **(i)** New leisure centre
Industrial estate (2 marks)

(ii) Two detailed reasons, road access, road junction, new housing nearby, close to parkland, green use of rural–urban fringe (2 marks)

(iii) Two disadvantages detailed, increase in traffic on road and junction, development of green land, attract further development (2 marks)

2 *Level 1 (1–2).* Basic understanding of the rural–urban fringe and why it is attractive to developers and people who live there.

Level 2 (3–4). Clear understanding of factors effecting development in rural – urban fringe and the quality of life for people who live there. (4 marks)

3 *Level 1 (1–2).* Basic ideas about redevelopment and inner city, some understanding of why the rural–urban fringe is developed.

Level 2 (3–4). Shows a clear understanding of rural–urban fringe and links with inner city.

Level 3 (5–6). Detailed understanding of impact of redevelopment in inner city and reduction of demand for housing/retail/leisure in rural–urban fringe, reasons described and explained. (6 marks)

4 *Level 1 (1–2).* Shows a basic understanding of the type of developments in the rural–urban fringe and conflicts between people.

Level 2 (3–4). Shows a clear understanding of the type of developments in the rural–urban fringe and conflicts between people.

Level 3 (5–6). Detailed understanding and description of impact of developments at rural–urban fringe and consideration of reasons for conflict e.g., local residents/ new housing sheet. (6 marks)

5 *Level 1 (1–2).* Simple ideas about chosen planning scheme, limited locational detail, limited reference to advantages and disadvantages, poorly located basic examples.

Level 2 (3–4). Gives a clear description of the planning scheme, identification of advantages and disadvantages, with reference to different groups, some understanding of change and conflict in rural–urban fringe.

Level 3 (5–6). Detailed description of advantages and disadvantages of scheme with reference to located examples, clear understanding of change/conflict in the rural–urban fringe and the management of change. (6 marks)

Chapter 5 – Unstable plate margins (pages 48–55)

1 a) *Level 1 (1–2).* Copies idea from resource and makes the point about loss of houses/ worry about safety.

Level 2 (3–4). Considers the idea in a broader way by suggesting that structures may be unsafe after an earthquake and that after shocks can occur. (4 marks)

b) *Level 1 (1–2).* Uses article to describe the damage and idea of homelessness, people forced from their homes. Some idea of other factors mentioned – crime/stress.

Level 2 (3–4). Describes all the impacts – damage/homelessness/crime/stress and begins to understand the idea of immediate and longer-term impacts. (4 marks)

2 a) *Level 1 (1–2).* Basic idea about plates and plate movement with limited development.

Level 2 (3–4). Shows a clear appreciation of the frictional movement taking place to create the sudden shock of an earthquake. (4 marks)

b) *Level 1 (1–2).* Describes a basic link to plates – idea that some areas are unstable and others not.

Level 2 (3–4). Clear appreciation that there is a link to plate margins but not all plate movements cause earthquakes – idea of destructive plates. (4 marks)

c) Points mark – three marks for any appropriate/relevant point. Points might include: magma chamber/vent/crater/secondary cone/magma tube etc. (3 x 1) (3 marks)

3 *Level 1 (1–2).* Shows a basic understanding with simple points about always having lived there/cannot move away/certain advantages

Level 2 (3–4). Gives a clear understanding of potential of areas in terms of soil fertility/ geothermal energy, etc. Ideas not well developed/limited exemplification.

Level 3 (5–6). Detailed appreciation of why people live in these areas. Brings in LEDC/ MEDC idea – lack of choice/management and positive advantages such as soil fertility/ climate/economic advantages. Some points developed through the use of examples. (6 marks)

4 *Level 1 (1–2).* Gives a basic description of impacts with little detail and no real explanation.

Level 2 (3–4). Uses examples to describe the impact of tectonic hazards and begins to appreciate why areas might be affected differently. Shows some understanding of primary/secondary effects.

Level 3 (5–6). Uses detailed located examples to make comparative points. Shows a sound understanding of the relative primary and secondary impacts in relation to MEDC/LEDC. (6 marks)

5 *Level 1 (1–2).* Basic ideas about either preparation in terms of building or making people aware of what to do. Limited depth in either area – simple descriptive points.

Level 2 (3–4). Gives a clear appreciation that buildings can be built to withstand earthquakes and some example of how. Brings in ideas about how people can be prepared and made aware of what to do – some description of earthquake practice days (Japan), etc.

Level 3 (5–6). Detailed appreciation of how buildings can be designed to withstand events with specific examples (steel frames/shock absorbers etc). Mention of human planning at both individual and government level, i.e. individual awareness/emergency services, etc. (6 marks)

6 *Level 1 (1–2).* Basic ideas that might include simple consideration of emergency aid (food, water, blankets, etc). Includes the key idea about keeping people alive. Largely descriptive – no real exemplification.

Level 2 (3–4). Clear understanding of needs after a natural disaster including food/water/medical help/shelter etc. Includes some locational or aid agency details.

Level 3 (5–6). Detailed appreciation of needs after a natural disaster which includes both emergency and longer term redevelopment ideas. Clear reference to specific aid agencies or examples. (6 marks)

Chapter 6 – Weather hazards (pages 56–63)

1 a) (3 x 1)
(i) Over 1000 mm
(ii) 600
(iii) Farming (3 marks)

b) *Level 1 (1–2).* Basic comments which tend to copy resource and identify immediate problems such as food/water, etc.

Level 2 (3–4). Clear observations which identify the need for immediate help (food/water/shelter, etc) and also longer term aid in getting infrastructure/schools/farming back together. (4 marks)

c) *Level 1 (1–2).* Basic responses which are based around lack of money/general poverty.

Level 2 (3–4). Clearer understanding which begins to consider the influence of development/infrastructure, etc.

Level 3 (5–6). Detailed appreciation of the influence of development and the general lack of services and investment. (6 marks)

2 *Level 1 (1–2).* Basic description which identifies winds as the main hazard with some mention of flooding.

Level 2 (3–4). Considers a range of hazards including strong winds, coastal and river flooding as well as other factors such as mudslides. (4 marks)

3 *Level 1 (1–2).* Basic consideration which picks up ideas in a superficial way and mentions simple climatic points. Tentative human links and limited locational exemplification.

Level 2 (3–4). Clear understanding that flooding can be caused by both physical (rainfall) and human factors (deforestation/building), etc. although not always balanced. Some locational context.

Level 3 (5–6). Identifies a number of factors which might cause flooding (climate/relief/development/deforestation, etc) and uses examples linked to appropriate points. (6 marks)

4 Accept a specific flood management scheme or a multi-purpose scheme which includes flood management.

Level 1 (1–2). Basic appreciation of flood management with descriptive comments which lack depth. Might name area but limited locational depth.

Level 2 (3–4). Begins to consider both advantages (control of flooding/safety) and disadvantages (cost/effect on other places, etc) but not always in a balanced way. Some locational context.

Level 3 (5–6). A number of clearly identified advantages and disadvantages linked to a specifically located flood management scheme. (6 marks)

Chapter 7 – Water and food supply (pages 64–71)

1 a) *Level 1 (1–2).* Basic points copied from resource with limited development. No clear appreciation of the difference between malnutrition/starvation.

Level 2 (3–4). Uses points to identify links in the chain and develops the links. Appreciation of the difference between malnutrition and starvation. (4 marks)

b) Any two points (2 x 2). One mark simple listed point (any appropriate point)
Examples include:

- Poverty
- Lack of land
- Conflict
- Agricultural change
- Poor transportation
- Overgrazing/over-cultivation
- Drought
- Pollution, etc.

The second mark is for some development. For example:
Poverty (1) means that people cannot buy food (2)
Drought (1) reduces the amount of food available (2) (4 marks)

c) Could be large-scale multi-use projects (such as the Aswan Dam) or smaller scale projects, including aid projects.

Level 1 (1–2). Basic ideas which might include simple references to irrigation/better organisation/scientific ideas. Lacks depth/detail and no real locational context.

Level 2 (3–4). Clear link between method and output 'Irrigation can improve the growth of crops and allow a greater variety to be grown.' Uses examples to make points – location variable.

Level 3 (5–6). Clear links between methods and outputs expressed through the use of well located example(s). (6 marks)

2 a) One mark – describes areas of semi-desert/arid areas
The second mark – clear understanding of process (2 marks)

b) *Level 1 (1–2).* Limited understanding of desertification and narrow focus that identifies either 'climate' or some appreciation of human factors.

Level 2 (3–4). Clear understanding of what desertification means with some reference to both physical and human influences, not always fully developed.

Level 3 (5–6). Detailed appreciation of desertification and clear understanding of how climatic and human factors (over-cultivation/overgrazing/removal of vegetation) work together to encourage desertification. (6 marks)

3 a) One mark – topsoil removal, etc.
Second mark – link to human impact (food/farming, etc.) (2 marks)

b) *Level 1 (1–2).* Basic ideas about better farming/more food, copied points from resource with limited development.

Level 2 (3–4). Clear understanding of the link between better food and improved diet leading to better health. Uses data well to develop broader ideas – bringing in ideas about improved health – less illness/lower infant mortality, etc.

Level 3 (5–6). Detailed understanding which goes beyond the resource and considers ideas like food surplus equals more time for other work – for example, selling food and products equals more income which equals better investment in housing/healthcare, etc. (6 marks)

4 a) *Level 1 (1–2).* Basic links to general health and mortality

Level 2 (3–4). Clear links to health and mortality with some appreciation about the impact of low levels of health or general living standards and economic development. (4 marks)

b) *Level 1 (1–2).* Simple ideas about building wells or describing schemes in general with limited depth.

Level 2 (3–4). Clear understanding of methods with some detailed appreciation of water supply schemes. Some locational context with named examples.

Level 3 (5–6). Uses example(s) that are well located and identifies water supply problems with a detailed description of how they are being improved. (6 marks)

Chapter 8 – Pressures on the physical environment (pages 72–79)

1 a) (i) A Swimming/sunbathing
B Any type of entertainment
C Birdwatching / fishing / photography (3 marks)

(ii) Level 1 (1–2). Basic ideas about the use of the beach for holidays and the lake for outdoor activities.

Level 2 (3–4). Clear appreciation of how the physical environment encourages specific types of tourism. For example, a sandy beach is good for sun bathing.

Level 3 (5–6). Detailed appreciation of how the specific characteristics of the environment encourage tourism. That is, a sandy beach with a gentle slope is safe for children. Or a lake on clay encourages a permanent habitat for wildlife, appealing to birdwatchers, etc. (6 marks)

b) *Level 1 (1–2).* Basic points about people/buildings with only limited development of the idea of 'pressure' on the environment.

Level 2 (3–4). Clear understanding that tourism has brought about change and this may mean damage to the environment. Specific examples used with some reference to Figure 1.

Level 3 (5–6). Detailed appreciation of human pressures on the landscape and land-use changes. Identifies specific detail from Figure 1. and makes clear reference to how human use might put the area under pressure. (lake/pollution/wildlife) (6 marks)

2 a) (2 x 1)
- To protect areas
- To encourage the use of recreational areas (2 marks)

b) *Level l (1–2).* Basic ideas about time/access/car ownership, etc.

Level 2 (3–4). Broader range of ideas including the range of opportunities in National Parks and increased awareness/use of the environment. (4 marks)

3 a) *Level 1 (1–2).* Limited understanding of conflict, tends to describe individual pressures (litter/damage to areas/gates left open, etc)

Level 2 (3–4). Clear appreciation of conflict and some example of how conflict might occur, e.g. walkers want to roam freely but farmers want to protect their land. (4 marks)

b) *Level 1 (1–2).* Basic ideas of pressure which might include things like litter/erosion/ congestion. Limited appreciation of management. No real locational detail.

Level 2 (3–4). Clear idea of the links between use and pressure and some management ideas linked to locational detail. Often single ideas not fully explored. (Carparks/litter bins, etc.)

Level 3 (5–6). Uses examples to explain in detail how areas are being managed. Development of management, i.e. Traffic pressures; …'increased use of public transport/park and ride schemes/restricted parking, etc. (6 marks)

4 (a, b) *Level 1 (1–2).* Named feature of erosion/deposition with a basic understanding of process which lacks detail.

Level 2 (3–4). Clear understanding of process and uses some terminology to explain how a named feature is formed. Credit use of diagrams. (4 marks)

Understanding and explaining conflict (page 78)

The key to this question is to identify the needs of particular groups and then to suggest why their particular activities may conflict.

There are a number of possible conflicts on the diagram, including:

Tourism	↔	**Angling**
Tourists want to be able to wander freely, may make a noise and use the river. They may drop litter in the river.		Anglers want peace and quiet and don't want the fish or the river disturbed.

Walking Walkers want to be able to walk freely in the hills and enjoy the peace and quiet of the countryside.	↔	**Shooting** People who shoot want areas of land protected from walkers for reasons of safety. This often takes up a great deal of land.
Farmers Farmers have to earn a living and need to be able to graze their animals. They don't want their animals disturbed or frightened away.	↔	**Tourists/Walkers** Tourists/walkers want the freedom to move about freely in the area, but may disturb the wildlife and drop litter

Chapter 9 – Contrasting levels of development (pages 82–89)

3 a) (i) – Japan
(ii) – Bangladesh
(iii) – Japan (3 x 1) (3 marks)

b) *Level 1 (1–2).* Limited understanding of what the data really means with tentative suggestions about links between people/doctor, adult literacy and general development.

Level 2 (3–4). Clear understanding of what the data means and how it is linked to development with some development which considers either health or education impacts.

Level 3 (5–6). Detailed understanding of both indices and links with development. Both sets of data developed to include links with health and living standards and education/training opportunities. Observation about amount of money countries can spend on services. (6 marks)

c) *Level 1 (1–2).* Basic points which are largely descriptive comments about the division and make simplistic observations about 'rich' and 'poor' differences.

Level 2 (3–4). Clear ideas which suggest that there are often differences within continents and even within countries and that other data is required to get an accurate picture. (4 marks)

2 *Level 1 (1–2).* Basic observations about countries being more developed and largely descriptive points about what this means (more money/jobs, etc).

Level 2 (3–4). Some clear reasoning which offers an explanation. i.e. Some countries have more resources/better communications/more power/broader range of industry/better education and training, etc. (4 marks)

3 Interpret living standards in the broadest sense, improvements to health, education, services, employment, housing, etc.

Level 1 (1–2). Basic understanding of what constitutes living standards with some general points which might suggest improvements. 'Better health care, improved sanitation', etc.

Level 2 (3–4). Clear understanding of what constitutes living standards and develops links between improvements and living standards. 'better sanitation would improve health levels and reduce disease'. Some locational context with use of examples.

Level 3 (5–6). Uses specific examples (aid schemes, self help, government schemes) general economic development) to explain how improvements to incomes/facilities/services can improve living standards/conditions. (6 marks)

Using data in examination questions (page 88)

a) Japan
Kenya (2 marks)

b) *Level 1 (1–2).* Basic points which identify that the higher incomes have higher life expectancy. Limited reasoning about increasing wealth resulting in higher living standards.

Level 2 (3–4). Identifies the relationship between wealth and life expectancy but mentions the slight anomalies in the relationship, using examples from the data. Developed idea which links wealth to better facilities (healthcare, etc) which might increase life expectancy. (4 marks)

c) *Level 1 (1–2).* Basic point about it only being one idea or an average which is not always reliable. Limited use of the data to express that the relationship between GNP($) and the other data is not always clear.

Level 2 (3–4). Clear observations about GNP $ being an average which does not always reflect general facilities. Uses data to demonstrate this point by expressing the relationship between GNP ($) and other data. (4 marks)

d) *Level 1 (1–2).* Limited understanding of what infant mortality actually is, some mention which identifies ideas about child death with tentative links to other factors.

Level 2 (3–4). Clear appreciation of what infant mortality is and how it is often linked to wealth (use of GNP$). Some exemplification of the causes of higher infant mortality and links this to general living conditions.

Level 3 (5–6). Detailed understanding of what is meant by infant mortality and use of data to express links with other factors. Good understanding of causes of high levels of infant mortality and brings in other linked living standard ideas such as diet, education, healthcare, water quality, housing conditions, etc. (4 marks)

Chapter 10 – Resource depletion (pages 90–97)

1 **(i)** Former USSR
(ii) North America
(iii) Western Europe (3 marks)

b) Two reasons (2 marks)

2) a) Water (1 mark)
Oil, gas (1 mark)

b) Forest (1 mark)

c) *Level 1 (1–2).* Two ways stated, basic.

Level 2 (3–4). Clearly described, for timber, for tourism. (4 marks)

3 *Level 1 (1–2).* Basic ideas about resource extraction and damage to the environment, limited exemplification.

Level 2 (3–4). Clear understanding of the links between resource extraction/use and environmental damage, examples used.

Level 3 (5–6). Detailed description and ideas developed, clear use of examples. (6 marks)

4 *Level 1 (1–2).* Basic ideas about use of resources and ways of reducing consumption, simple ideas about recycling, appropriate technology.

Level 2 (3–4). Clear understanding of need to reduce resource consumption and contribution of recycling or appropriate technology in reducing use, some ways suggested.

Level 3 (5–6). Detailed consideration of ways in which either recycling or appropriate technology may reduce resource consumption, explanation. (6 marks)

Chapter 11 – Economic development and the global environment (pages 98–105)

1 a) Africa (1 mark)

b) North America (1 mark)

c) *Level 1 (1–2).* Basic ideas about global environmental damage, causes, of damage, contribution of carbon emissions.

Level 2 (3–4). Clear understanding of ways in which global environment is damaged and the part played by carbon emissions.

Level 3 (5–6). Detailed description of ways in which carbon emissions can contribute to global environmental damage, understanding of sources of emissions and damage. (6 marks)

d) *Level 1 (1–2).* Basic statements/ideas about reducing emissions.

Level 2 (3–4). Clear development of ideas about ways in which carbon emissions can be reduced.

Level 3 (5–6). Detailed understanding of sources of carbon emissions and ways in which emissions can be reduced. (6 marks)

2 *Level 1 (1–2).* Basic understanding of sea level rise, limited development of how people can be affected.

Level 2 (3–4). Clear understanding global warming/sea level rise and impacts on people.

Level 3 (5–6). Detailed understanding of global warming/sea level rise links and the varied impacts on people globally. (6 marks)

3 *Level 1 (1–2).* Basic understanding of global economic development and a sustainable strategy.

Level 2 (3–4). Clear understanding and description of one sustainable strategy in global economic development.

Level 3 (5–6). Detailed description and explanation of a sustainable strategy in global economic development. (6 marks)

4 *Level 1 (1–2).* Basic understanding of pressure groups, and the ways in which environmental groups influence people.

Level 2 (3–4). Clear, detailed consideration of ways in which environmental pressure groups may influence governments. (4 marks)

Chapter 12 – Tourism and the economy (pages 106-113)

1 a) Thailand (1 mark)

b) *Level 1 (1–2).* Identifies named examples from the map with some appreciation of global differences (most in Asia).

Level 2 (3–4). Clear reference to the area between the tropics and differences between the three main continents. Some reference to the density of holiday centres in Asia. (4 marks)

c) *Level 1 (1–2).* Basic points which may be general and not always related to LEDCs – more money/greater access, etc.

Level 2 (3–4). Specific links to LEDCs which might include comments about climate/ scenery/increased availability/awareness/encouragement of LEDC as part of development process. (4 marks)

2 a) One mark – looking after environment idea
The second mark – some understanding of sustainability/long term protection. (2 marks)

b) *Level 1 (1–2).* Basic description which tends to describe what it is rather than a locational example. Limited understanding of why it is ecotourism.

Level 2 (3–4). Uses an example to describe how it protects/looks after the area. (4 marks)

3 *Level 1 (1–2).* Basic idea of physical features which might include weather/beach areas, etc and some basic description. No real locational detail.

Level 2 (3–4). Explains how some areas have developed based on physical factors such as climate/beach/mountains, etc. Links to type of holiday development.

Level 3 (5–6). Detailed understanding of how physical factors have encouraged tourism across a range of examples which might include beach/mountain/natural scenery/ wildlife, etc. (6 marks)

4 *Level 1 (1–2).* Basic understanding of economic links which brings in jobs/money. Focus might be either advantages or disadvantages.

Level 2 (3–4). Clear understanding of economic links with examples of jobs and some appreciation of linked jobs. Has both advantages and disadvantages (may not be balanced) and some locational examples.

Level 3 (5–6). Uses examples to explain how tourism can bring economic advantages (jobs, business improvement to services, transport, etc) and also disadvantages (seasonal jobs, lower wages, etc). Good understanding of both advantages and disadvantages using examples. (6 marks)

5 a) *Level 1 (1–2).* Limited use of example and basic understanding of 'environment pressure'. Lists points such as pollution, litter, etc.

Level 2 (3–4). Clear and appropriate example and good understanding of how tourism can damage environment, e.g. erosion/damage to vegetation/wildlife, etc. (4 marks)

b) *Level 1 (1–2).* Limited reference to an example and tend to describe problems with only tentative management ideas.

Level 2 (3–4). Uses an example to describe what is being done to protect areas.

Level 3 (5–6). Uses an example to describe what is being done to protect areas and explain how the measures might work in the long term. (6 marks)

Revise your map reading (pages 114–115)

1 Southfield farm (1 mark)

2 8979 (1 mark)

3 a) Industrial estate
b) Place of worship/tower (2x1) (2 marks)

4 a) South-west
b) South-east (2 x 1) (2 marks)

5 a) 3
b) 4 (km not required) (2 x 1) (2 marks)

6 Contour lines and spot heights (2 x 1) (2 marks)

7 *Level 1 (1–2).* Identifies slope (contours) and two rivers. Use of height.

Level 2 (3–4). Describes slope – even slope running down from hilltop (heights used). River in south in a valley. (4 marks)

8 *Level 1 (1–2).* Identifies the named features (motel, industrial estate, crematorium) with limited development or use of the key.

Level 2 (3–4). Identifies the named features and broader key-based features (roads, different width, general built-up area, television masts, etc.). (4 marks)

Index